Coping With Family Violence

Coping With
Family Violence

by
Morton L. Kurland, M.D.

THE ROSEN PUBLISHING GROUP, INC.
New York

10-12-88

Published in 1986 by The Rosen Publishing Group
29 East 21st Street, New York City, New York 10010

First Edition
Copyright 1986 by Morton L. Kurland, M.D.

Library of Congress Cataloging-in-Publication Data

Kurland, Morton L.
    Coping with family violence.

    Includes index.
    Summary: True stories in various settings and situations depict child abuse and other
kinds of violence between family members.
    1. Family violence. 2. Child abuse. [1. Child abuse. 2. Family violence] I. Title.
HQ809.K96 1986   362.8'2   85-31249
ISBN 0-8239-0677-9

Manufactured in the United States of America

About the Author

Dr. Kurland is a psychiatrist and also a family man. Married for thirty years, he is the father of four daughters, two of whom are married and have children of their own. All were raised in southern California and graduated from Palm Springs High School.

Dr. Kurland was trained in Kentucky and New York City. He was a member of the full-time faculty at the New Jersey Medical School, formerly called Seton Hall College of Medicine. He has also lectured at Rutgers University, Princeton University, the University of Alabama, the University of Iowa, and several other institutions. He has given a great many talks and seminars at hospitals and medical centers around the country.

Dr. Kurland originally practiced in New York and New Jersey, but moved to California in 1971. At present, he is the Chief of Psychiatry at the Eisenhower Medical Center in Rancho Mirage and the Medical Director of the Barbara Sinatra Children's Center, which is part of the Eisenhower medical complex. In addition, he is the psychiatric consultant to the Betty Ford Center for alcohol abuse and is on the consulting staff at Angel View Crippled Children's Hospital and Desert Hospital in Palm Springs.

He and his wife live with their two younger daughters in Palm Springs.

Acknowledgments

The author wishes to express his gratitude to those people who, in their own ways, have made possible the completion of this work.

First to Ruth Rosen, who has acted as a perfect editor, encouraging, positive, and only once in a while deleting some probably too graphic passages. Also to another Ruth, Ruth Scott, who has been more than a typist. Her quickness, feel for the material, understanding of the field, and especially her diligence in preparing an almost perfect final product have got to be an author's dream.

Technical, informational, and in-depth case material as well as background were freely given by both John and Bonnie Shields. John, Executive Director of the Barbara Sinatra Children's Center at Eisenhower, and his wife, Bonnie, who is in charge of therapeutic programs for the Center, gave freely of their knowledge and experience, especially in the area of sexual abuse.

The founder and inspiration for the Center, Mrs. Frank Sinatra, deserves all of our applause for devoting so much of her time, energy, and resources to provide a practical platform from which to mount the struggle against violence to children and adolescents. Her work and that of her husband and the members of the Board of the Eisenhower Medical Center should set an example for public-spirited citizens across the land to pitch in and defend and support those who cannot do it themselves, the victims of family violence.

Finally, the author wishes to acknowledge that none of this book would have seen the light of day without the hard work, support, and practical proofreading, organizational ability, and drive of Adrienne M. Kurland, R.N., his wife, partner, lover, and best friend.

Morton L. Kurland, M.D.

Contents

Introduction

"Violence, like charity, often begins at home. The roots and the causes of violent activity in people's lives frequently lie in their earliest experiences. It is well known that acts of aggression and assault go from generation to generation, and that dealing with the problems that arise from violent activities among members of families really means dealing with the families themselves and understanding them from generation to generation."

This book deals with the violent confrontations that occur in otherwise ordinary appearing families. Everyone is potentially a victim of someone else's anger, rage, confusion, and fear. It can start in the earliest days of infancy with mothers who are afraid of children, don't know how to raise them, feel inadequate to the task and overwhelmed. It continues with parents who don't know how to control young children, because the children are too active, too energetic, too precocious, or because the parents allow them to get out of control. Later, violent activities can occur among children in the same family. Sometimes psychiatrists refer to this as sibling rivalry. Often it is the kind of violent action that occurs when an argument gets out of hand and one brother hits another, or one sister destroys another's property.

Ultimately, the violence can extend to the children themselves, who begin to attack their own parents.

All of these kinds of violent activities have causes and, of course, terrible effects. If we can begin to understand the causes, we can begin to deal with preventing them. There are ways to change people who engage in attacks on other people. There are sources of help, understanding, and shelter. We attempt in this book to describe some actual cases of people who were caught in the storm of rage and anger, confusion and fear that brings about attacks on others. We try to show ways in which these problems can be understood and handled and help can be obtained.

The names of the people have been changed, but the stories are true. The settings can be in a big city, a country town, or anything in between. The cases can happen in this country or elsewhere. The situations can happen to anyone. Any of our readers might be involved in this kind of problem, and the help that is described is available to all of them if they know where to look for it.

Coping With
Family Violence

CHAPTER I

Battered Children

Ann B. was a high school student of sixteen when she first realized that she was pregnant. She was afraid of having the baby and of taking care of it, and at the same time she was afraid to do anything about it. She had been involved in what she felt was a love affair with a boy on the football team in her high school. She believed she was safe from becoming pregnant because she understood the "rhythm" method of contraception. Either she wasn't counting right or the "rhythm" was not what she thought. The next thing she knew she was pregnant and afraid to tell anyone.

As the pregnancy progressed, she did tell her boyfriend, Tom, and he said that he would do the "right thing" and marry her. They had a long discussion with their families, and it was agreed that the two should marry when Ann was five months' pregnant. Tom had to leave school and take a job in a local supermarket. Ann decided that having the baby was the best thing to do at the time. She went through with her pregnancy although it was painful and uncomfortable for her, as she wasn't prepared for it.

"I was scared all the time," she later said. "I didn't know what was going to happen or how I was going to take care of this new baby. I felt the baby moving inside of me and was scared that it would hurt me."

Ann had been scared most of her life about a lot of things. When she was a small child her parents had thought her unruly and mischievous. They had punished her by hitting her with belts and rulers and sticks and anything else that came to hand. She always felt that she might be doing something wrong and tried to make sure she didn't make any big mistakes. She was afraid of both of her parents, who believed that the only way to control her was through punishment. They had learned this from their own families, and it probably went back for many generations. Ann grew up scared and stayed that way. Her relationship with her high school sweetheart was a way of her avoiding her family and their criticism.

Although there was a mental health clinic and a family counseling center in her town, Ann never sought guidance. Her family didn't believe in those things. They held that everybody had to solve their own problems. They didn't like ''nosy'' outsiders getting involved in their business. Ann felt more alone than ever as the day of her delivery came closer, and she was afraid she would be hurt by her labor and the birth of the child. As it turned out, it was a long labor, and she was in a lot of discomfort for more than a day before the baby was born.

After the baby was born, he cried a lot and needed a lot of attention. Ann was so frightened by everything going on around her that she didn't have enough milk to feed the baby. She had to learn to make formulas and sterilize bottles, and she didn't get much help from Tom, because he was so busy working at the store and so tired when he came home at night.

Besides, Tom was mad at her underneath; he really hadn't wanted to get married and have a family, and he never had a chance to play football in his senior year in high school. He had always thought he could be a star and and go on to college, but he never had the chance to find out.

All in all, there was a lot of anger and disappointment in their household. They had rented a small apartment a few blocks from Ann's parents because it was all they could afford. Ann didn't want, under any circumstances, to live at home, and her family didn't particularly want her with them. They considered her a bad example for the other children because she had got pregnant and hadn't been married until she was "five months gone."

The troubles with the baby began immediately with his crying and her not knowing what to do. She thought she could never satisfy him, and eventually little Tom seemed to her a burden. When he finally was a year old she had learned that she could prop his bottle on a pillow, and feeding him all the time kept him from crying so much. Even so, he did cry a lot because he wanted to be picked up and held and rocked. Ann never felt comfortable with that and didn't do it very much.

"There are probably a lot of girls who shouldn't be mothers," she said. "I guess I am one of them. I never really liked playing with babies, and I never liked baby-sitting for my little brothers and sisters." She had always felt uncomfortable with small children, and now that she had one of her own that was her total responsibility, her fear and anxiety became even greater. She was always afraid that she would make a mistake, or that the baby would get sick, or that she would be blamed for something terrible happening. When he cried for attention she tried to ignore him and turned up the volume on the television so that she couldn't hear. The noise became deafening sometimes, and then Tom would come home and get angry. He didn't very much want to play with little Tom either, because he was tired and still so mad at both Ann and the baby.

By the time the baby was a year old, he was toddling and breaking things and making a mess everyplace. Ann had to follow him around and try to prevent him from wrecking her house entirely. Tom would come home and call her sloppy, and careless for not making supper, and an anchor around his neck.

"I guess I wasn't cut out to be a wife either. I think Tom was mad at me most of the time, and finally I got mad at him and the baby too. That's probably what led to most of my trouble with him."

Ann came to believe that little Tom was a nasty child and destructive and "probably evil." She figured that the best way to handle him was to spank him. Her parents had always said, "Spare the rod and spoil the child." She decided she wasn't going to have a spoiled child, so she began to spank him when he pulled on things and knocked things off tables and made messes. When little Tom had trouble controlling his bowels and she had to constantly change diapers, she got mad at that too.

"Why couldn't he learn I wasn't a housemaid to go around and clean up after him and change his dirty clothes all the time. I was only seventeen years old. I was supposed to be at the beach swimming and surfing.

I wasn't supposed to be stuck in a little apartment with a whiny baby with snot running down his nose.''

Ann was bitter and angry as she recalled how she became more and more violent toward her child. She began to hit him when he cried, and when he tried to ask for things she would slap him in the face. Finally, her anger became greater and greater, and so did her violence. Her husband noticed that the child was becoming sullen, withdrawn, and scared. When Tom tried to pick him up, the child backed away and cowered in the corner. He cried when either Tom or Ann came near him. Tom realized that Ann was probably being too rigid and strict with the child, but because he was mad at both of them for ruining his life, he didn't think much about it.

It was only when Tom's sister, Betsy, came to visit them that she noticed what was happening. She herself was sixteen and wanted to be part of the family. She enjoyed children and wanted to play with the baby. When she saw how he backed off and cried and whimpered, she knew that something was wrong, but she wasn't quite sure what it was.

One day Ann asked Betsy to take little Tom to the doctor for ''his shots.'' The pediatrician asked her what was the cause of the welts on little Tom's buttocks and thighs. He said he thought somebody was hitting the child, and Betsy realized that this was probably so. She confided in the doctor some of her fears and some of her observations. The doctor told her that he was required by state law to report to the authorities any suspected cases of child abuse. This meant that he had to file a medical statement with the county department in charge of "Child Protective Services." He examined Tom and sent in the report.

Later, a social worker came to visit Tom and Ann. Tom was very angry when the worker came one evening unannounced, showed her identification, and said she had been sent to investigate his family. Ann was equally angry and outraged, and argued loudly. When the social worker finally told them that she suspected a violation of the law and that the doctor had reported it, Ann felt betrayed.

Finally, it became clear that significant injury was being done in the family, and the matter came to court. There were several visits with the family, and finally a judge ordered that little Tom be placed in a foster home with other parents who were paid by the county to take care of children in such situations.

Ann and Tom appeared in court and were ordered to seek help in a family counseling service.

Ann was placed in a group called Mothers Anonymous, women who had similar problems with their children and who got together regularly to talk about how they dealt with the children and how they could overcome the problems.

Tom was assigned to a similar group for fathers. During the course of group therapy, many of his own problems and feelings were expressed by the other fathers, who ranged in age from seventeen to thirty. Many of them were angry at their wives for getting pregnant. Others didn't want to be responsible for a family, and many of them felt that they were over-

worked, overtired, and overburdened by family activities. They wanted to get out and play and have fun,
and they had to come home and take care of a wife and
child or children. They themselves sometimes got angry
and explosive and had little patience, either with their
wives or children.

Tom eventually talked about some of his own feelings
and found out that they were similar to those of the
other guys in the group. Most of them were sorry that
they had married and wished they had joined the Navy
or run away from home and had never assumed responsibility.

"It was too late for that," Tom said. "I guess we all
realized that we had got ourselves into this fix and now
we had to do something to handle it. The group helped
me a lot, and I found I wasn't the only one who felt
that way. I'm glad that I had to join the group, and I
hope it will help me to deal with my child and my
responsibilities as I get older and maybe grow up a little
bit more." The group had been very helpful to Tom.

With Ann it was a somewhat different story. She
attended Mothers Anonymous but never felt that she
had the same problems as the other girls. She felt that
she was different and that they didn't understand her,
didn't care about her. She had trouble telling them how
frightened she was most of the time. Even though many
of them talked about how they had been punished and
severely treated when they were children, Ann never
admitted to any of these feelings.

Finally, the group therapist decided that Ann needed
individual attention, and she was referred to a psychia-

trist who consulted with the group. After a number of individual sessions in which she came to know the doctor and realize that he wasn't picking on her or judging her or considering her dumb or inadequate, she began to trust him a little. When he told her that she seemed to be scared, she admitted that she was. She began to talk about her experiences and to develop some insight into her life.

After almost a year, she admitted that she was glad she didn't have the baby with her and said that maybe someday she could grow up a little more and assume responsibility. It was then that she said perhaps she never should have had a baby and that lots of girls probably shouldn't be mothers. The doctor told her that there are lots of girls who should be mothers but only when they grow up themselves. Ann was far too young to have a baby and be responsible for it. She was far too scared to take care of a child and had little information about the responsibilities of caring for another life. She might still make a fine mother, but she had a lot to learn and a lot of growing up to do.

It was probably the most painful admission in her life, but Ann finally agreed that it was good that little Tom was in a foster home with people who knew how to take care of him. She thought that maybe someday she would be able to do that, but it was a long way in the future. She agreed that it was a good thing there was a law requiring doctors to report physical abuse of children so that steps could be taken. She also finally admitted that she was glad Betsy had told the doctor what had been going on, because otherwise the problem could have become more and more serious and she might feel even more guilty and overwhelmed than she did already.

Help is available for people who either find themselves in this situation or see friends or relatives involved in it. Mental health clinics and family guidance clinics exist all over the country, with trained social workers, mental health workers, psychologists, and psychiatrists who have a great deal of experience with this kind of problem. Many of them are available either free or at minimal cost because they are sponsored by the United Way or some other agency. The important thing is to find out where this help is available and to reach out for it. Sometimes the family doctor can be a useful source of information. Clergymen often know these resources, as do school teachers and counselors in high schools and colleges. A person who suspects something owes a responsibility to the child involved as well as to friends or family to take action which, in the long run, can be the most positive thing he or she has ever done.

CHAPTER II

In the Land of Giants

Many times violence in families is treated by the family as normal. Sometimes it is even justified as necessary to "control" the behavior of children. This can continue even when children are adolescents and young adults. The constant assaultiveness of parents eventually is reflected in more ways than one in the behavior of the battered children.

Teenagers are frequently embarrassed to discuss their difficulties at home and feel "weird" when they have to reveal things that have happened to them that they know to be out of the ordinary. One of the big problems is that many adolescents fear that the battering they receive from their parents, especially their fathers, is in some way their own fault. They have grown up constantly being told by their parents that they are bad, "worthless," "selfish," "thoughtless," and a number of other negative ideas that are probably not true. Often the terms used against them would better fit their parents, but the young people are not aware of that. Children grow up surrounded by people who are two, three, and five times their size. To a child of four or five, parents appear to be giants. Actually, insofar as small children are concerned, the parents really are giants, and they are Lilliputians. Lilliputians were the tiny people of the land of Lilliput in Jonathan Swift's story *Gulliver's*

Travels. Gulliver was shipwrecked in their land. The little people were terrified by his size and tried to control him because they feared he would destroy them. When we are little children, our parents seem like male and female Gullivers and we the tiny beings who may be crushed by their footsteps. Later, as we get to be teenagers and perhaps grow even larger than our parents, we still carry a mental image of ourselves as small children, and we act accordingly. As a result, parents continue to attack, batter, and physically beat their children even when the children are in high school or in college.

Harvey D. was fourteen and in his first year of high school. He began getting into trouble at school because he was acting out in a negative way against his peers. He picked on other boys in his class and sometimes girls as well, and got them involved in fights. He usually picked on kids who were smaller than he. Sometimes he tripped people as they walked out of the classroom and then challenged them to a fight if they got angry. Other times he purposely soiled other kids' clothing or threw snowballs or mudballs at them, or spitballs in class. He sometimes smeared up their homework papers or in other ways damaged their possessions.

Most of the time, the other children would fight back and lose because Harvey was careful to pick on people he thought he could beat. Besides, Harvey was pretty good at fighting and seemed to be able to take care of himself physically. Although most of the kids didn't want to be "squealers" and tell on Harvey, it soon became evident to the teachers and some of the older kids in the class that Harvey was a bully. Some of the bigger boys, upon whom Harvey didn't pick, decided that it was up to them to defend the smaller kids against Harvey's bullying and teasing. As a result, Harvey was sometimes forced into fights with boys his size, and he sometimes got the worst of it.

Finally, one of the bigger boys decided, after a fight with Harvey, that he ought to talk to somebody about the situation. Roger had a good relationship with the basketball coach, since he was trying out for the team, and he stayed after practice one day to talk to him about Harvey. He told the coach why he had been involved in fights with Harvey and something about Harvey's behavior in general.

The coach was pleased that Roger had told him about Harvey's problems, and he then arranged to have a talk with the counselor for the freshman class. In most high schools each class has a counselor to advise students on academic choices, programs, careers, and the like. The counselors usually are also trained in psychology and have a degree in counseling. This particular counselor was so trained and recognized that Harvey had a significant problem. He realized that help was needed before Harvey hurt someone, parents complained, or for some other reason Harvey was expelled or got into trouble with the police.

Harvey was asked to visit the counselor, and since he had no choice in the matter, he did so. At first, Harvey denied that he had been in any fights or had trouble with any of his peers. When the counselor said that he had several witnesses and comments from more than one teacher, as well as the coach and Roger, Harvey admitted that possibly he had been involved in some fights.

"I just feel that I can't let people get away with things. They're always picking on me and looking to find my weak spots," Harvey told the counselor. "I know that you can't let people get the better of you. Once you show them that you're weak, they'll walk all over you. My dad told me that, and he told me that I had to be tough. I'm going to be tough, and I'm not going to let those pantywaist mama's boys put anything over on me."

It became clear that Harvey was turning things around; instead of admitting to himself that it was he who was challenging people to fights and inciting the trouble, he tried to place the blame on the others. He truly believed that he was the victim, not the one who started the trouble.

The counselor felt that it was important to clearly document what was going on, and he asked Harvey's teachers and classmates to keep him informed of Harvey's activities and what went on with him in the school and playground over a period of time.

The reports came back that Harvey continued to stir up trouble, to get involved with smaller kids, and now even some girls, in fights and arguments and even petty thievery. The counselor called Harvey in again and said that he now had documentation for Harvey's responsibility in these matters. He was not surprised, however, when Harvey continued to deny all and to project his feelings onto other people and blame them for what was happening. This is sometimes called a paranoid position, which means that a person is not willing to accept his or her own shortcomings and prefers to blame negative feelings on others.

The counselor realized that Harvey's problem required professional intervention, and he called on the school psychologist to became actively involved. The psychologist asked Harvey's parents to come in and discuss matters with her, as she wanted to give Harvey some tests and needed their approval. The parents were reluctant to come in at all and failed to keep several appointments. Finally the counselor spoke to both of them on the phone and said that if they did not come in, Harvey was in danger of getting into serious trouble.

The father and mother both turned up at the appointed hour for the next interview and were extremely defensive about their son. They said that Harvey had always had problems, that they had done their best to control him and had never spared the rod. They said he had been given plenty of whippings and that his obstinacy was something they had been dealing with since he was a small child. They were very defensive and denied responsibility for anything negative that he had done. Said the father,

"We've done everything that we know how to do to keep him in line. I never let him get away with anything, and I keep pushing him to do the right thing. If he's gone bad, it's probably because of the influence of the other kids here at school, because we keep him in line at home. If you people don't know how to do your job, that's not my fault."

The father became increasingly angry as he harangued

the psychologist and seemed about to erupt in violence of his own.

Mrs. D. said that she agreed with her husband and added, "There's no way that anything Harvey's doing is our fault. We keep him in line, and he never had no trouble before this. Nobody ever complained about Harvey. He watches his P's and Q's or he knows the reason why. Anything that's going on here is not our doing."

The psychologist tried to explore the defensiveness of the parents, but they were unwilling to admit that their attitudes and feelings had any relation to Harvey's picking on little kids or getting into trouble. They did say that they would take punitive steps if they had any proof, and they challenged the psychologist to "prove it" and let them handle the matter in their own way.

The psychologist was reluctant to give them any proof, fearing that the consequences to Harvey would be disastrous. She said, however, that she would like to do some testing that might in some way clarify the issue. The parents reluctantly agreed to allow Harvey to undergo psychological testing and even some counseling if it didn't cost them anything.

"Maybe some kind of counseling would help straighten out his little brain. God knows, we've tried everything that we know how," said Mrs. D. "We don't think he's so bad, but if there's even the slightest truth to what you're saying, then you do whatever you can, and if you can't do it, we'll make sure that he toes the line."

Eventually, the psychologist did give Harvey some tests, including the well-known Rorschach test. In this procedure the person looks at a series of ink blots of various shapes and colors and gives his impressions of what they mean, perhaps even telling a story about the pictures he sees in the ink blots.

In doing this test, the psychologist was not surprised to find that Harvey was a very frightened young man most of the time. He saw giants and monsters and devouring creatures in the ink blots, indicating that he was very much afraid and saw himself as weak and helpless. It was not surprising that he needed to pick on kids smaller than himself or weaker, because he felt so helpless and overwhelmed most of the time. It also became clear in the test that Harvey was terrified of his father and, to some extent, his mother. He saw them as huge, overwhelming and destructive people, almost like monsters who were going to destroy him.

The psychologist felt that it was very important to get Harvey into counseling, and she undertook to do some of the counseling herself while awaiting approval of the family to send him to a child guidance clinic.

When Harvey got into regular therapy with a mental health worker whom he trusted, he was able to reveal the feelings that he had indicated on the Rorschach test: that he was terrified most of the time and picked on other kids as a way of overcoming his phobias and fears about weakness, helplessness, and vulnerability. As he felt safer with the counselor, an attitude of trust began to allow Harvey to be more understanding of the world and feel less like a Lilliputian. If he could learn to relate to the counselor in a more normal way, he might come to learn that not all adults were overwhelming, powerful, and punitive thinkers. A long-term therapeutic relationship would allow Harvey to know that some people were thoughtful and kind and considerate. He would find that some people were even interested in helping him to learn, to like the world around him, and to make his own way in it without the need for force and violence.

The lesson to be learned in dealing with problems such as Harvey's is that many kids who become violent with their peers are reacting to lessons they have learned at home. Often parents are extremely punitive and violent, probably repeating what they learned in their own childhood. If the cycle isn't stopped, it is quite likely that kids like Harvey will grow up and do the same things to their kids that were done to them. Violence begets violence; that is, people who are treated violently become violent themselves. They pass it on to the next generation, and it doesn't stop unless there is a forceful and meaningful intervention. Somebody has to break the cycle.

Probably the best way to help in stopping such a vicious cycle is to be aware of the resources available. Often there are knowledgeable people in authority who can take action. The chain of events in Harvey's case is not an unusual one. If someone in the peer group has the courage and understanding to talk to a responsible adult, that can be the best beginning. It is not squealing to report somebody who is doing damage to others. It is the height of responsibility to act as an adult even when you're a teenager. There is nothing wrong with "blowing the whistle" on someone who is committing a foul. In sports, the referee is there to prevent cheating and to allow the game to be played properly. If there were no referee calling fouls and blowing the whistle, the game would eventually deteriorate and there would be no winners or losers—just total chaos and no fun at all.

In life then, somebody has to blow the whistle and alert the referee. In school it may be useful to talk to a trusted teacher, whether it be a history teacher, an English professor, a track coach, or a member of the administration staff. He or she can call on school counselors and psychologists who are specifically trained to deal with problems. They, in turn, are able to distinguish between kids who have major psychological problems brought about by family difficulties or long-term learning disorders and those with immediate situational problems that can be resolved with a simple discussion or two and do not involve long-term therapy. The decision is then up to the experts, in consultation with the involved adolescent and his or her family.

In any event, then, it is important to know that it's okay to ask for help and to know where to go for help. Besides an authority in school, sometimes the family doctor, the clergyman, or a concerned relative can be helpful. Most communities have child guidance clinics, adult mental health clinics, and other facilities that are available even if one doesn't have the resources to pay for psychiatric treatment on a long-term basis.

The important thing to learn is that while we may start out as Lilliputians in a land of giants, we all do have the opportunity to grow and someday become the giants. When we do so, we have to know how to treat the Lilliputians as real people who someday will grow and mature just as we have.

CHAPTER III

Caught in the Crossfire

One of the hardest things for young people to realize
in dealing with their families is that their parents are only
people after all. As we saw in Chapter II, children sometimes see their parents as giants in a physical sense and
feel at the mercy of these huge creatures. Besides physical
size, young people often feel that their parents are intellectual giants as well. To a small child, both mother and
father have had so much experience in living that they
appear to know everything. It seems as though they can
do no wrong, that everything they do and think and feel
is not only right, but exactly right. The parents assume
an aura of omniscience; that is, they seem to know everything and understand everything, especially what is going
on in their child's mind.

This is not surprising, since from the earliest days of
infancy the child's mother knows when he needs to have
his diaper changed or when he is hungry without the
child's ever having to speak the words, "I am hungry,"
or "I feel dirty," or even "I want to be held and cuddled."
The mother seems to know this by some magical power,
so it is frequently the case that children feel that their
parents know everything there is to know.

It is small wonder, then, that when parents begin to
squabble and fight it is hard for young people to understand

that it may be the fault of their mother or father or both. When this kind of trouble begins, the young people tend to believe it is *their* fault. Somehow, they believe, they have done something wrong and that is why their parents are squabbling. They feel that they haven't been good enough. They get the impression that if only they had done the right thing, the trouble never would have come up. They look into themselves and try to find ways in which they have behaved badly. They try to handle things differently. If the arguments and fights continue, they try even harder to search their souls to discover how they have gone wrong and caused the difficulty.

When family squabbling reaches the point of physical violence, the child may be overwhelmed. When the child is an adolescent, he or she sometimes tries to intervene physically between the parents, feeling guilty and therefore responsible for stopping the trouble. Obviously, it is rare that this can occur. For the most part, all that happens is that the child gets caught in the crossfire of the conflicting emotions of the parents.

Jeffrey B., when first seen in psychiatric treatment, was fifteen years old and a sophomore in high school. He was a student in a boarding school to which his parents had sent him because of the apparently insoluble problems that had arisen at home. Jeffrey was very unhappy in the school and began to act in destructive and foolish ways. He cut classes. He failed to do his homework. He began to make jokes and inappropriate remarks in school. His grades were terrible; even though he was extremely bright, he was failing in almost every subject.

It became clear to his teachers that Jeffrey was a very unhappy young man emotionally and troubled by things other than his academic career.

In Jeffrey's first sessions with the psychiatrist, he related that his parents no longer lived together, that they had, in fact, separated the year before he came to boarding school. He remembered that all the time he was in elementary school his parents were in constant conflict. He couldn't recall a time when they were not fighting. He remembered that his mother was a very ambitious and energetic woman who wanted to create a career for herself. She had been going to college, taking graduate courses toward a professional degree. Jeffrey's father was a successful manufacturer of plumbing supplies. He had never gone to college, but he pointed out in his wife's frequent attacks about his lack of education that he knew enough "to make a very good living for all of us." Jeffrey thought that his father felt inadequate because of his mother's constant pointing out that he didn't speak good English, that he didn't understand music or literature, that he was not acceptable in the social circles to which she aspired. At the same time, his father was angry at the mother's pretentiousness and her need for acceptance in social circles in which he could find no special merit. Jeffrey remembered his father saying on many occasions, "Why do you need to hang out with all those stuffed shirts? They're a bunch of eggheads. They couldn't think their way out of a paper bag. They're all phonies, and you're a phony just like them." Jeffrey remembered his mother's becoming angry and accusing his father of being too passive and allowing people to take advantage of him because of his poor education.

He remembered one particular night when his mother became so angry that she slapped his father in the face with her open hand. Jeffrey was terribly embarrassed for his father. When his mother hit his father a second time, the father hit her back. They came to blows, and both were bruised and battered after a few minutes of fighting. Jeffrey was only nine years old, but he remembered feeling that he had to stop it. He tried to get between his parents, but they simply pushed him aside.

Later, as the arguments persisted and the trouble became even more serious and more dangerous, his mother became angry at him. She accused him of telling relatives and friends about their fights. She even threatened to hit him with a horsewhip if he didn't stop "spying on me." She actually never struck him with the horsewhip, although she did hit him with her hand on a number of occasions when he tried to argue with her and prevent the constant conflict between his parents.

Jeffrey felt overwhelmed and helpless in this situation. He had no place to turn, nowhere to go for assistance. When finally he had a chance to talk to his grandmother on his mother's side and tell her how he felt about what was happening in his home, he agreed to go and stay with her for a few weeks. Unfortunately, Grandma felt that she was too old to take care of the needs of a teenage boy, and he was sent to the boarding school.

At that point he felt totally abandoned, not only by his angry mother but by his father as well, who didn't attempt to rescue him. Even his grandmother, whom he had trusted, agreed that the boarding school was probably the best solution. Jeffrey never liked the school and never liked not being at home. He never liked having to perform in a competitive academic situation with other kids who were "always trying to prove how smart they were but who probably were in just as much trouble in their own families as I am," he later said.

It became clear that Jeffrey's academic failure was really related to his feeling of rejection and to an unconscious effort to fail, to be tossed out of the boarding school, and eventually to return home in one last effort to patch up his parents' marriage.

For some reason, the parents had decided that sending Jeffrey to boarding school would solve their problems. They began to share Jeffrey's delusion that he had some responsibility for their poor marriage. Jeffrey had, in fact, become the scapegoat for his parents' troubles. Their arguments initially had nothing to do with him, but ultimately, because he had tried to intervene, he became the focus of their struggle. They finally decided that if he were away they would get along better. Of course, that wasn't so, and within a year they separated physically: They had mentally separated years earlier.

When a young person is trapped in a struggle between parents, he feels helpless and overwhelmed, with no one to whom he can turn. After all, his parents are the two most important people in his life and the two people he has depended upon for as long as he can recall. No one could be closer to him, and when they are struggling with each other, he is forced either to side with one or the other or to maintain an uncomfortable and unrealistic neutrality.

There are no easy solutions for problems as complicated and serious as these. It is rare that one parent is totally at fault and the other blameless. Most of the time, people create mutual problems and aggravate them one with the other. It is important, however, for young people to gain a perspective on what is going on. First of all, it is essential to understand that it is extremely rare for a child to be the cause of parents' marital discord. The parents, after all, are the adults. The child, by definition, is not yet mature and hasn't had the experience of life that the parents have already gained. Thus the parents are the ones who have to make the "mature" judgments and choices, and the child is the one who has to learn from them. For the child to blame himself is obviously inappropriate, and it is even worse when the parents in turn blame the child.

Jeffrey recalled frequently feeling overwhelmed with guilt at the thought that he might have said something during one of the arguments to make it worse. He remembered feeling that maybe his mother *should* have hit him with the horsewhip because perhaps he really had said something to friends or relatives that he didn't recall. He believed that he never talked about family troubles outside of the home, but when his mother accused him of doing so, he felt that "possibly or maybe even probably she was right"; after all, she was his mother and knew so much more than he did.

When Jeffrey finally had the opportunity to talk to someone whom he felt he could trust and who had no ax to grind, he began to feel more comfortable. Possibly his grandmother could have played that role had she been strong enough and patient enough to go through it with him. She, however, felt overwhelmed, and after all, she was so close to his mother that she could not be unprejudiced and unbiased in trying to help him to understand the situation.

In one session with the psychiatrist, Jeffrey told about a time when his English literature teacher had assigned a book report on a famous novel. Jeffrey decided to make a parody of the assignment, writing it like a science-fiction story, hoping thus to attract attention and interest and, at the same time, become a special person. He didn't realize at the time that he was saying very little about the book, had no real understanding of it, and kept drifting off the topic to make jokes and crude comments in his report.

When he was told by his teacher that his work was totally unacceptable and that he had no chance of passing the course, Jeffrey wasn't really very much upset. He said he was surprised but that actually it showed him that if he did his work poorly enough and "if they thought I was really crazy enough, maybe they wouldn't let me stay here anymore. Maybe they'd call my parents or even my grandmother and tell them that I had to be sent home. I really didn't want to stay here. I don't like it here, and I don't think anyone else likes me either. I've probably messed up things here just as badly as I messed up my family at home."

It became clear that Jeffrey still hung onto the belief that he was responsible for his family's troubles. Since they had done nothing to disabuse him of this notion and, in fact, had encouraged it, it wasn't surprising that he felt responsible for being unwanted and unloved. He had done nothing to gain the confidence and friendship of his fellow students or to get involved in activities at school because his primary goal was to get kicked out as quickly as possible.

One of the goals of the psychiatric intervention was to help Jeffrey to understand that he had to make the best of his situation, that it was not his fault but was in fact his responsibility to make the best of it.

After regular hour-long sessions twice a week for several months, Jeffrey finally came to agree that he could, in fact, make friends, that he was potentially a likeable young man and actually was talented, bright, and clever. For starters, he began to make friends with his roommates, stopped playing pranks on them, stopped being an intellectual snob, and began to feel more comfortable with everyone. His problems were by no means solved and, in fact, they continued for some time; but he began to get a handle on the idea that it had not been his fault that things had gone so badly and that it was up to him in the future to make his life work better.

He began to write more positive letters home, letting his family know that things were going better and that he actually enjoyed being at school. His parents came to see that Jeffrey was not the core of their problem nor, indeed, did he have much to do with it. They began to look for assistance and ultimately obtained professional guidance to help them straighten out their lives.

After several years they were able to reconcile their differences and to live in greater harmony.

By this time, Jeffrey, too, had learned some greater harmony, and as he neared graduation from prep school he was able to consider going to college and making a career of his own. He learned to respect his father's industriousness and cleverness and forbearance in the face of his mother's overwhelming ambition and drive. He began to respect his mother for her brightness and intellectual abilities, which he had inherited. Most important, however, he began to see both of them as actual people.

Jeffrey realized that his parents were human beings. They were not magical figures who happened to have the title of "mother and father," but actually individual persons who had been young and had fallen in love. They had created a child without having had any parenting experience at all. They made the kinds of mistakes that many people make in growing up, and they were not especially mature when Jeffrey was a kid. This led to his being trapped between them and becoming a victim of their sniping at each other.

Jeffrey was actually caught in the crossfire of two unhappy people. When he began to see them as individuals and not as revered, magical figures, he began to understand what had gone wrong. He began to forgive himself for believing that he was responsible for all of their troubles, and to realize that there were ways to deal with these problems through understanding, through thoughtfulness and kindness, and through his own efforts to make his life worthwhile.

Ronnie T. had a similar problem in being caught between his parents and their rage. In Ronnie's case, a lot of the trouble had to do with his father's drinking problem. Ronnie's father would come home from work at 8:00 or 9:00, quite drunk. His mother would become angry and berate the father for being late, for not having supper with the family, for being sloppy and confused, and the father would react with rage.

"It almost seemed as if my mother was trying to make him mad. She would say things to him when he was drunk that everyone in the house knew were going to make him angry." Ronnie could see that his mother was baiting his father and causing him to become so explosively angry that violence would result. Ronnie and his two younger brothers were present during most of the conflicts and arguments. Sometimes they would hide in corners or run up to their beds and "make believe that we were asleep." Many times things would be thrown; glasses and bottles and even pieces of furniture would go crashing around downstairs as Ronnie and his brothers hid under the covers. They felt helpless and overwhelmed by the struggle between these two people whom they loved and upon whom they were totally dependent.

Ronnie was the oldest of the children and felt that it was up to him to lead the way in helping to solve the problems in the household. It is not uncommon for a young boy to feel that, in some way, it is up to him to save the situation. Much like the case of Jeffrey, Ronnie felt that it was somehow his fault that his parents fought. If he could only find the key to the problem, it wouldn't continue. He had to discover some way to keep his father from being angry and attacking his mother. He had to find some way to make his father stop drinking and be more reasonable. He also had to keep his brothers from being scared and to protect them, because it made his father angry if they cried or whimpered or showed in any way that they were unhappy during the fights their parents had with such regularity and intensity.

When a child is caught in this situation, sometimes the only thing he can do is fantasize that someday he will grow up and solve the problem. When Ronnie first began to cope, he was only ten years old. He realized that he didn't have the strength to intervene between his parents. ''The only thing I was able to do was to imagine what it would be like when I grew up and got strong enough to get in between them and stop the fighting.''

Ronnie didn't seem to have many other choices, and there was little or no intervention available in the family or in the community when he was nine or ten years old. Later, when he was in his early teens, his father began to attend meetings of Alcoholics Anonymous, and the entire family went to a group called Alanon. Ronnie participated in these meetings and learned that there were other kids and other families with similar troubles.

He considered running away from home on a number of occasions when he was eleven, twelve, and thirteen but felt that he had the responsiblity to protect his brothers. He also felt that running away would only get him out of the conflict, leaving his parents in the core of their problem.

Ronnie and his professional counselor discussed the question of running away and agreed that it doesn't change anything. It may be true that "He who fights and runs away lives to fight another day," but it isn't usually an effective solution for adolescents. They don't have a base of operation; they don't have a source of income; they don't have an adequate education; and they don't have any experience with which to cope with the problems of a complicated society. If there is a relative who is close and understanding and who can take the kids on for a time while the parents struggle with their problems, sometimes that can be a temporary solution.

When the problem is alcohol, of course, there are many other complicating factors having to do with the health of the alcoholic, the addiction to the drug alcohol, and the behavior that it causes in the drinker. The children in the family became victims of the parent's substance abuse, and if the nondrinking parent is not able to take steps to help, everyone can be adversely affected. Often an uninformed parent becomes a "co-alcoholic"; by not taking a firm stand against the substance abuse, he or she in some way encourages it.

The belief that the drinker can stop whenever he chooses is wrong. Intervention is essential. Sometimes even the adolescent can alert other members of the family, such as aunts, uncles, or grandparents, to become aware of the problem, which they may wish to deny. A clergyman, a family doctor, or a concerned friend can be helpful in calling attention to the problem.

It is not "squealing" to inform some concerned adult about the situation in the family. Even when the child is not being physically attacked or abused by the violence between the parents, he is emotionally injured. A father or a mother who gets drunk and attacks the spouse can injure the child just by the example of the violence. Children are emotionally injured by seeing their parents hurt each other and, in addition, are influenced to inflict the same kind of injury on their own husbands or wives when they grow up. Every effort must be made to stop violent behavior as early as possible, and young people themselves need to explore avenues of help if they find themselves caught in this kind of conflict.

Resources are, in fact, available in the community. In a situation like Jeffrey's, in which a young boy is literally exiled from his home because of the parents' conflict and inability to resolve it, his best recourse is to consult with members of the family, especially grandparents, uncles, and aunts, who he feels may be able to intervene between the parents and get them to find the assistance they need or, failing that, to resolve the problem by divorce, if necessary. Sometimes it is better to break up a marriage before someone is hurt than to stick together and have constant warfare. Obviously, the solution of reconciliation, understanding, and counseling is the most desirable one if it can work.

In a case such as Ronnie's, the intervention of someone who understands about alcoholism is the most fruitful choice. Most communities have branches of Alcoholics Anonymous or Alanon, or Alchol Awareness Clinics that can be used by parents with problems of this nature. Sometimes a teenager's school counselor can put him in touch with someone who knows about these things. Some members of Alcoholics Anonymous are willing to come to the home and talk to the drinker. If the young person makes the contact, the discretion of the A.A. member can be trusted not to reveal the source of the information. It can be very embarrassing for a child to talk about these problems to strangers, and yet, sometimes it is the only way to get matters resolved. If these kinds of facilities are not available, friends and relatives can reach out and find help for the parents. The important thing in all of these situations is that the adolescent or child should not be caught in the crossfire between the parents, because he or she can be injured terribly. It is better to yell for help than to be wounded. It is better to seek counseling than to run away. It is better to try to succeed than to fail purposely as Jeffrey did.

Although young people are not responsible for their parents' troubles, they are ultimately responsible for their own happiness; if they can find a way to get someone else to dampen the fires of their parents' anger, they can help themselves as well.

CHAPTER IV

"Dad Loves Me More"

In the sixties there was a television program starring the Smothers Brothers that enjoyed great prominence for several years. One of their favorite lines was one brother saying to the other, "Mom always loved you more." This was a running gag on the show and brought a lot of laughter. It struck a responsive chord in many people, however; that kind of feeling exists frequently in families. Rivalry between children for the affection of the parents is common. One brother blames another for having been cheated of parental affection, and similar struggles among sisters are even more common.

A hundred years ago, Sigmund Freud, the father of modern psychiatry, described what he termed the Oedipus complex, a personality phenomenon in which the young child develops an affinity for the parent of the opposite sex. That is, a young boy is fascinated by his mother, and the young girl is interested in being like her mother only to gain affection from the father.

Frued's theory was based on a tragic play by Sophocles in which the Prince Oedipus was abandoned as a child by his parents. Returning to his home town as an adult, he unwittingly killed his father in a sword fight and later married his mother. Learning the truth years later, Oedipus put out his eyes in despair. He paid the price for his incestuous relationship with his mother, even though he never knew that she was indeed related to him.

Freud believed that unconscious incestuous desires exist in every family, with the young boy wanting to overwhelm the father in order to possess the mother for himself. He also believed that the reverse is true and that young girls want to have their father for themselves and get rid of the mother. He called this the "Electra complex," after another Greek mythological figure.

In these days, we don't necessarily believe that there is a sexual yearning for the opposite parent, but there is no question that young people are interested in their parents in the sense of wanting all of their attention and affection. This is frequently the case with teenage girls, who feel that their mother is trying to push them away from the father and keep him for herself.

Irma was a forty-five-year-old mother of a teenage girl, Betty. She sought psychiatric counseling because she felt that Betty was "out of control." She complained that Betty did not listen to her and fought with her all the time, that Betty was "boy-crazy" and wanted only to run around with her high school friends. Betty was seventeen and a senior in high school. There was no question that she was growing up and becoming interested in young men. Irma feared, however, that Betty's interest was more than just a passing one and that her intense feelings about young men were going to get her in trouble. She came to the psychiatrist to talk about this and, in effect, ask the psychiatrist to change Betty back into the sweet child that she had been ten years earlier.

"Betty was always such a good child. She never got into trouble, and she always listened to me," Irma said. "I never had any trouble with her, and she always played with nice children from good families. I never thought she would grow up to be such a hell raiser. I'm not sure how I went wrong."

Irma was preoccupied with the feeling that she had made some major mistake and that Betty was growing up to be a "loose" young woman. What she meant was that she feared Betty was becoming so "boy-crazy" that she was forgetting her principles and everything her mother had taught her, hanging around with a bad crowd and bound to get into trouble.

"I know that she must be smoking dope by now. Even though she denies it, I can tell. I smell that honey smell in her car. She tells me it's from 'clove cigarettes,' but I know better. I'm sure she's been smoking dope, and hanging around with that crowd that she does, it's not surprising. What can you do to stop her?"

Irma was filled with anxiety that Betty was going to go bad and that the whole family structure would collapse. "God knows, I've tried everything I can. I try to cajole her and to bribe her and give her things, but that doesn't work. I try to restrict her and keep her away from her friends, but that's even worse. She sneaks out at night and hangs out with all of those terrible people. Her father's no help either. He doesn't seem to care, and she knows that she can always go to him and get him on her side. I'm doing everything I can, and I've turned to you to give me advice. What can I do?''

Irma said that Betty had been a good student in school and received average grades, but even these, in her senior year, were beginning to slip a little. She felt that Betty was too interested in running around to worry about grades and achievement and might even drop out of school unless something were done. She asked the doctor to intercede and talk with Betty and try to find out what was at the core of her problem.

It became clear after two or three visits that Irma was obsessed with her daughter's behavior and that it was likely that she was exaggerating the situation. Finally, Betty was invited to come in to tell her side of the story.

Betty was attractive and quite articulate. She was able to present a clear picture of how she saw things, and of course it was quite a different view than that of her mother.

''My mother has always been a wet blanket. She doesn't want me to do anything. She sent me to special schools in elementary years to keep me away from kids that she thought were from the wrong side of the tracks. She wanted me always to be a goody-goody, and I guess I was most of the time. Now that I'm in high school and a senior, I can see that there's more to life. I can't live the kind of life that my mother wants me to live. She wants me to be a bookworm and to get all kinds of good grades and to go to church and to be a goody-goody and never to have any fun. She thinks that I'm going to turn out bad, and if she keeps pushing me the way she does, maybe she'll be right.''

Betty was filled with righteous indignation. She felt

that her life was being controlled by her mother, or at least that her mother was trying to control her life. She believed that her mother really didn't care about her interests and wishes, but only in how she looked to the community.

"She says to me all the time, 'What will the neighbors think, what will Mrs. Jones think, what will Mrs. Smith think, how will Mrs. Gunther talk about us in the Woman's Sodality?' " Betty felt that Irma's only interest in her was as a reflection of herself and what effect Betty's behavior would have upon Irma's social standing.

"My mother just sees me as some kind of symbol. I'm supposed to be the one to represent the family to everyone else. Why doesn't she worry about herself? She's always talking to me about smoking dope and being an embarrassment to her. Why doesn't she think about how she looks when she drinks too much at some of her cocktail parties? I know my mother gets smashed at least once a month and maybe more. She doesn't think there's anything wrong with that, I guess. But if I have one or two friends that she doesn't like, I'm on restriction. It isn't fair. She's trying to control me and to prevent me from doing the things that she probably wants to do herself. I just can't stand that woman any more, and as soon as I'm eighteen I'm going to leave!"

Betty was obviously very agitated and concerned at what she felt was her mother's attempt to control her future and everything she did, just as she had controlled her past and her activities when she was a child.

"I'm not a little kid anymore. I don't have to do

what my mother tells me. When I'm eighteen, I'm going to be legally an adult. In the meantime, I know enough about life to take care of myself. I don't have to listen to every little thing she says. My father isn't so concerned. He knows that he can trust me. It's only my mother who thinks I'm an evil person.''

It was true that Betty's father did not seem to be as concerned as the mother. He never kept the appointments that were made for him, saying that he didn't have time because of his busy schedule. He owned his own business and probably could have made time if he chose, but he didn't regard the situation as a major problem. He apparently saw it more as a struggle between his teenage daughter and his wife.

''I know my father is on my side. He doesn't allow her to pick on me all the time. He helps me sometimes in arguments. When she gives me a hard time about money, he sometimes slips me a twenty-dollar bill, and she doesn't even know it. I hope you won't tell her. What I tell you here is in confidence, isn't it?''

After being reassured that everything that one tells a psychiatrist in the office is one's own business and will be revealed only by consent, Betty went on.

''I know that my mother is jealous of me. She sees me as being the way she was when she was seventeen or eighteen. She is afraid I'm going to go wild the way she probably did when she was my age. I know a lot about her that she doesn't think I know; her sister told me. She was a wild kid. She actually left home when she was sixteen and never went back. She married my father when she was only seventeen herself. For some reason, she doesn't trust me. She's afraid that I'm going to make the same mistakes that she did when she was my age. I'm smarter than that. I'm smarter than she is. She'll see.''

It was clear that the situation was a classic "Electra complex" between Betty and Irma. Indeed, when she was presented with this idea, Irma did agree that Betty was very much like her, "a carbon copy of me when I was seventeen." She remembered that she drank and wanted to run around too much and that she got into fights with her own mother. She did, in fact, run away from home. She never finished high school, because she married Betty's father when she was seventeen. Betty thought that was probably because she was pregnant, and Irma confirmed it later on.

"In those days, you had to do that kind of thing. There was no such thing as living with somebody or having a baby out of wedlock. I had to marry him, but I wanted to anyway. It's been a good marriage. We've been together all this time, and we've never had any trouble between us until Betty started going crazy. I think it's the teen years in our blood. I guess my mother was the same way. I know I was. We've got to do something for Betty, though, so that she doesn't go wrong. I know you understand and that you'll be able to help.''

It was decided that the situation required outside help. It was clear that mother and daughter were not going to be able to resolve their problems without assistance from a third party. Irma already knew this, and Betty agreed that she wasn't able to change her attitude either.

Mother and daughter came to the doctor together for an hour's visit. The family therapy might have worked better if the father had come too, but he made himself unavailable.

As it turned out, there was increasing tension in the home, which at one point came to physical conflict. Irma accused Betty of having marijuana in her car; she said thàt she had smelled it and was never more certain of anything in her life. Betty denied it, and the two began to argue. At one point, Irma pushed Betty, and Betty grabbed her hand to stop her, saying, "You can't do that to me!" It was then that Irma grabbed Betty's hair and pulled it. Betty screamed and ran out of the house. She went to her dad's office and "told on" her mother. This created even more tension in the family when the father came home later and told Irma that he thought she was out of control herself and that she should "know better." Irma began to feel that nobody understood her or cared for her, and she became increasingly agitated.

It became clear that both sides needed to talk more and have less physical confrontation. It was agreed that Irma would see the doctor alone for an hour every week, to work out some of her feelings of anger toward Betty and, at the same time, try to understand why they were so strong and where they came from. Betty, at the same time, agreed to see a school psychologist so that she could express her feelings and not feel that she was constantly being criticized and picked on. As time went on, there were fewer episodes of yelling and screaming and no further violent attacks.

Irma came to see that she had identified Betty as a younger version of herself. She saw Betty as having her own personality and temperament and was really trying to redo herself in a perfect mold. She recognized that she had had problems as a teenager and had never accomplished everything that she wanted. She wanted Betty to graduate from high school and go to college. She wanted her to have a profession or some special trade or skill that would make her stand out. She wanted Betty to marry a doctor or a lawyer, not just a businessman as she had done. Her ambitions for Betty were really the ambitions she had had for herself earlier in her life but had never fulfilled.

As treatment went along, it became easier for Irma to talk about these things. She was able to accept the fact that she had done very well in her own life and had made something of herself despite her failed ambitions. She also came to recognize that Betty was a separate person and had the right to have her own ambitions and desires and make her own choices.

At the same time, as Betty began to have more confidence in the school psychologist, she was able to understand that her mother had trouble seeing her as a separate identity. She also learned that it was not a good idea to play her father off against her mother, as she had been doing for so long. She began to try to make her mother an ally instead of an enemy. She began to talk to her mother about some of her feelings other than angry ones. Her mother softened her views toward Betty, and Betty was able to see that her mother was just a person after all.

Eventually, Betty graduated from high school; although she wasn't an honor student, she did reasonably well. She was accepted at one of the state colleges and continued to see a counselor there for reassurance.

Irma continued to see the psychiatrist, but less often. She began to feel better about herself and more comfortable with her role in life. The father never did come in, but he was willing to support the treatment financially and emotionally and recognized that he had some part to play in the problems. It was not the most ideal solution to the difficulty, but it worked out reasonably well. Rarely is there an ideal resolution to any problem. The main thing is to learn to cope with them so that they do not destroy you. It is also important to avoid physical violence, which can lead to angry feelings and of course physical damage.

In this situation a positive outcome was possible because of the ability of both parties to listen, to understand that they were not the only ones with feelings, and to be able to make compromises in their positions.

CHAPTER V

"You'll Wreck My Stuff!"

Most children grow up in families in which there are other children. The "only child" in our society is more of a rarity than a commonplace. Of course, an only child has problems of his own, but one he does not have to deal with is sibling rivalry.

Families rank themselves according to the age of the children, the oldest child being the first born, the next child the second, and so on, with the youngest child always being seen as "the baby." Each of these positions in a family structure has meaning and has an effect on the individual child. If you were the first-born child, you have recollections of being the baby for a period of time and then giving way to the next child in line. If you were the youngest child, you never knew a life without older siblings and never had anybody younger than you to pick on or to push around.

For the most part, significant problems arise when there are multiple children because of the position of the children and the rivalries that result.

Usually the first-born child is seen as the favorite of the parents. Even Sigmund Freud was seen by his mother as "my golden Siggy" because he was her first-born child. Though others came, she always expected the most from Sigmund.

Although first-born is a favorable position to enjoy, it creates a lot of problems. First of all, one has to live up to the expectations of one's parents.In trying to do so, eventually you reach the point at which the expectations of the family become your own. You begin to expect even more of yourself than others expect of you.

As you go on in life, this continues. You can be forty or fifty years old and still act like the oldest child, of whom the most is expected. You can demand it of yourself even when you are doing very well, or as well as could be expected. This can create a kind of obsessive-compulsive personality structure that creates internal tensions and pressures. It also creates problems among your brothers and sisters, who may resent you, feeling that you were always the favorite and had the best of things. They compare everything to you and try to take advantage of you if you are the oldest.

Another problem for the oldest child is the arrival of the next one. If you are two or three or four years old, you are used to being the only child. When your mother becomes pregnant and tells you that you are going to have a baby brother or sister, you can become very angry. Nobody wants to yield his position as the only child. No one wants to have someone else take the limelight and get all the attention. No matter how much your parents try to sugar-coat the pill, it is a bitter one to swallow. You are giving up your favored position to an interloper. A new person is coming in to take your mother's time and attention. The new baby absorbs your mother's energy and concern; she doesn't have as much time to talk to you or tell you stories or play with you.

Even though she tries to give you both attention, it is inevitable that the infant demands more of her time, and that causes great resentment. Sometimes an older child becomes very angry at the baby. Cases have been known in which older kids try to injure babies, ignore them, or allow them to hurt themselves. Later this can create tremendous guilt for the oldest child, remembering how she or he became jealous, angry, and even destructive toward the baby.

The problem compounds itself when there is more than one sibling. If there are two or three other children, the oldest still resents the arrival of the next one, although it becomes less of a shock each time. But the next kid down the line can be angry at the arrival of a new baby taking away the limelight.

The second child, who is frequently the "middle child" in the family, is often pushed around a good deal by the oldest sibling. That kid may then resent the older brother or sister, and rivalry and anger develop between them. The younger child has to strive even harder to overcome the stigma of being always smaller, always less smart, always less aware of what's going on than a sibling two or three years older. This child may have to work even harder in school to outdo or rival the other. Sometimes the smartest thing to do is to avoid direct rivalry and choose other fields of endeavor. If the oldest child is a great athlete, the star of the track or basketball team or a cheerleader or a tennis whiz, the next child may decide to go in another direction. He or she may become a scholar or a debater, or pursue some other intellectual activity in order to excel in an area that has not been occupied by the first arrival.

The problem, of course, is compounded even further when a third or fourth or fifth child comes upon the scene.

For the sake of understanding, let us assume that there are three children in a typical family, but even if there are four or five, the scenario remains essentially the same: The youngest child becomes "the baby." The youngest child has a number of advantages, a tremendous one being that the parents are more experienced. When adults marry and have children, they are frequently in their early twenties or even younger. They have never had any experience in marriage or in having children. The techniques of raising a family are known to them only through their own experiences in growing up. Sometimes their teachers—their own parents—were good teachers and sometimes not. As a result, they learn by "on-the-job training." The first child is their first product and sometimes has to deal with a lot of parental mistakes. This is true to a lesser degree for the second child. The later children have the advantage of the parents' greater experience, which always helps in the growing up. The parents are older and more mature. They are more knowledgeable and calmer in dealing with the children and tend to be more liberal. They allow the younger children a lot more freedom than they did the older because they know how far they can go. They demand less and expect less of the younger children, having seen what the limits are with the others. This favors the younger children in many ways. They feel that they are loved for themselves and not for what they can do. The youngest child is often the favorite for these reasons and also because it is usually the last planned child and the last "baby" that will be around. This creates a lot of love and warmth, which is not unnoticed by the child. It is, of course, also noticed by the siblings, and that creates rivalry, anger, and resentment.

A drawback of being the baby, aside from the possible anger of the older children, is that the youngest child has to have greater motivation than the older ones because less is expected of him. Youngest children are often not expected to perform at the same level as the others. They know they can get away with a lot more and don't have to try as hard. For them to feel good and be successful in their lives, they need a great deal more motivation from others or from their own nature than do the others who have had this drummed into their heads all their lives.

Let us examine a three-child family in which some of these problems resulted in trouble and see some ways in which the adolescent can cope with the problems.

Arthur, Billy, and Sally were siblings in a middle-class family. Arthur was the oldest and when first seen by a psychiatrist was twenty years old. He was bright but shy and slight of build, and he was considered by his siblings as their mother's favorite. His brother Billy pointed this out over and over again and used to tease Arthur about it.

Billy, the middle child, was born three years after Arthur. Thus, Arthur had been an only child for three years until his brother came along. Arthur still remembered resenting Billy's taking his place as the baby and he remembered teasing him and pushing him around for years. It wasn't until Arthur became a teenager that he quit picking on Billy and teasing him physically. True, by that time Billy was ten or eleven and able to take care of himself. Billy was more muscular and stronger than Arthur had been at a comparable age. He was athletic and bright and always trying to outstrip Arthur in everything. Sometimes Billy and Arthur fought. While the parents broke up the fights when the kids were little, by the time Billy was eleven and Arthur was fourteen, Billy could hold his own. In a few years he began to be able to take Arthur out any time he wanted. As a result, Arthur stopped picking on Billy at all, and Billy came to feel that he could control Arthur physically if he needed to. This did not create good feelings within Arthur, who grew to hate Billy, or at least feel that he did.

The third member of the family structure was Sally. She was born four years after Arthur and was always seen as the baby. Her mother even called her ''Baby.'' Sometimes Arthur and Billy teased her, but for the most part neither of them saw her as a rival in their struggle for power and control. However, both of them saw her as the favored and spoiled child.

Sally saw Arthur and Billy fighting all the time, and she tried to stay away from this kind of violence, as it scared her. She wasn't especially pretty, but she knew how to relate to people and worked very hard to be accepted by the others. She knew, because of her status as the baby, that people would love her if only she would smile and be charming and that she would always get along with everyone because of this.

Arthur first visited a counselor when he was twenty years old and in college. Both psychologists and counselors were available in Arthur's school. He went to see one because he was becoming more and more obsessed with the fantasy of killing his brother. A fantasy is, of course, an idea that grows in one's mind; even though it doesn't come to pass, it can seem real and be frightening. Arthur had constant visions of beating Billy to a bloody pulp. Sometimes he would imagine running him over with a steam roller, sometimes hitting him with a baseball bat. He never intended to act out these feelings, but he was frightened because they seemed so strong and so real.

Arthur was able to describe these fantasies to the counselor and drain them off to such an extent that they were less frightening as time went on. Nevertheless, whenever Arthur returned home from college, he was frightened that he might get into it with Billy. Something terrible could happen. Billy, of course, was still in high school and starting to "feel his oats." He was on the high school baseball team and was strong and muscular. He thought that not only could he beat Arthur in a fight but probably was smarter as well. Arthur was beginning to have trouble in his college work because of his preoccupation with his rage toward his brother; at first, he didn't realize that he was also angry at Sally for being the baby and the favorite as well.

After a number of months of individual counseling, the counselor suggested that Arthur get into "group therapy." The group he joined was composed of twelve students in various years, eight boys and four girls. A number of them had similar feelings about their siblings.

One of the things that were talked about in the group was controlling anger, being able to talk about it and understand it without acting it out.

Many of the members of the group were very reassuring to Arthur because they had had similar experiences with brothers or sisters. They too were filled with similar kinds of rage and angry fantasies. None of them had ever carried out the violent attacks that they dreamed about, but all had fought with their brothers and sisters as they grew up. It became very important to them to understand that the kinds of physical fights one gets into at ages six, seven, and eight are not possible at sixteen, seventeen, and eighteen when you are much more capable of hurting each other. Struggles between adults have to be confined to words and avoid physical combat. The group came to understand this more clearly and to be less frightened of the possibility that they would ever act upon their fantasies.

Arthur finally got to the point of being able to come home on summer vacation and talk to Billy and Sally about the group. He told them about the feelings that had caused him to enter it and was surprised to learn that they had similar feelings about him. Sally told him that she had always resented the fact that he was the oldest and mother's favorite. She said she thought he was so much smarter than she that she could never equal his achievements in school and be as clever and as well known as he. She also resented Billy because he had been so successful on the baseball team. He was her particular target because he not only did well in sports but also had an almost straight A average.

"I always thought of you as being some kind of lucky

Joe. You seemed to have everything, Billy. You were able to do anything you wanted. The girls all liked you because you were so good-looking. You were strong, and you were smart. I never felt that I was good-looking, and I never thought that people liked me. It took me a long time even to tell you this. I'm really glad that Arthur has come home and gotten us together so we can talk about these things.''

Having a chance to express herself, Sally was able to unload a lot of resentment and anger to her brothers without feeling that she was a bad person. She found out that it wasn't terrible to talk about feelings as long as you didn't do anything to implement them.

Billy said that he too was glad Arthur had seen the counselor and joined the group because he had been thinking about it himself. He had read about group therapy, and a couple of his friends had been to see counselors. Since he didn't have any drug or alcohol problems, he didn't think he could get to see a counselor, but he wished he could. Billy didn't realize that you could see counselors about lots of other problems, including family difficulties, anger and resentment, fantasies, or even bad dreams. Billy might be able to get vicarious understanding of his own family structure and the rivalry between kids through others' experiences.

In the fall Arthur returned to college and to his group. He had become the senior member by this time and was able to be almost a ''co-therapist,'' giving the others the benefit of his experience of the year before. He now could tell them about how he was dealing with his angry feelings toward his brother and sister.

It is not unusual for people to have angry feelings about siblings because of the rivalries that are set up in the family. It is impossible for parents to love all of their children to the same extent. Even though all parents say that they love each child the same, anyone can see that that does not work out. It's sort of like the law: Everyone has the right to equal protection under the law, but not everyone is treated the same. Every child has a right to the love and affection of parents. Not every child is the same, however. Some are smarter and some are stronger. Some are weaker and some are more lovable. Some are short-tempered and some have difficulty in understanding. Some don't learn well and cause the parents to be annoyed. All of these factors enter into the way a child and his parents get along. Since there are likely to be several children and several problems among them, it is not surprising that all are not treated in exactly the same way. When a person becomes aware of this, he or she needs to try to deal with it on an individual basis. If the difference in treatment is great, it isn't inappropriate to talk to the other kids or even the parents about it.

Sometimes one child gets more time and attention because of particular deficiencies or inadequacies. This is hard for others to cope with and sometimes is very unfair. But it does happen, and as we grow up we have to learn to deal with it. If one child in the family has a chronic disease, it is likely that the parents will spend more time with that child. If one child has a mental disease or is mentally deficient or not as smart as the others, it is quite possible that the parents will spend five or ten times as much time with that child as with the others who are doing well. This is terribly unfair, but it is almost always the case.

It is often true that when one child gets into trouble with the law or with school authorities, or has similar problems, the other children receive less attention. They get less credit for being good than the other child gets attention for being bad. This is no excuse for the better children to disintegrate or, in resentment, to demand attention by acting out in a negative way themselves. It is important to talk to the parents about this and discuss it in a calm and reasonable way. Sometimes the intervention of a third party helps. Another adult, such as an uncle or an aunt, a grandparent, or even a friend, can help to point out to the parents what is going on. Sometimes that isn't enough, and a minister, a clergyman, a family doctor, or some other professional needs to come into the picture and point out to the family that ''the good kids'' need as much time and attention as do the others.

In the case of Arthur, Billy, and Sally, there was no good or bad kid, but mainly the normal kind of rivalry that goes on in families. On one occasion, Billy and Arthur got into a big fight. Arthur had been driving the second family car on an errand and had told Billy he would be back by seven o'clock so that Billy could use the car on his date that night. When Arthur didn't arrive until eight fifteen, Billy was furious. He threatened to pull Arthur out of the car through the windshield, and he grabbed Arthur by the shirt and tried to throttle him. The argument became heated, loud and explosive. The boys' grandparents were visiting, and the grandmother was so frightened that she called the police. By the time they arrived, Arthur and Billy had in effect resolved the argument and no one had been hurt. The police talked to the boys for a while and reassured the grandparents that this was not an uncommon event among boys and that no harm was done.

It is important to try to resolve such problems—who gets the car, who is using whose records on whose stereo, who is borrowing whose clothing—in advance. If someone breaks the rules and keeps the car longer, breaks a record, or ruins clothing, the other one has the right to demand some kind of repayment or reparation. It is never appropriate, under any circumstances, to become physically violent about a "thing." Things can be replaced. Records can be bought, and so can clothes. Cars can be repaired if they are dented, but people sometimes cannot. Hurt feelings can be mended, but broken bones sometimes don't heal properly.

It is never appropriate to attack somebody physically when you can deal with them with words. If it seems impossible to deal with another person on a one-to-one basis through conversation, a third party or parties may be necessary. There is nothing wrong with asking for help from a college or high school counselor. There is nothing wrong with asking for advice from a clergyman, a relative, or an older friend. This kind of intervention is the way to avoid trouble. This kind of solution is often the way to avoid long-lasting and even lifetime hatred, which need never start in the first place if it's handled properly.

CHAPTER VI

Early Marriage

"They tried to tell us we're too young,
Too young to really be in love.
They said that love's a word,
A word we've only heard
And can't begin to know the meaning of.

And yet, we're not too young to know
That our love will grow as years will go.

And then some day they may recall
That we were not too young at all."

Those are the words of a popular song written many years ago that still hold true today. Many people fall in love and want to marry, leave home, and start their own family as soon as possible. Often, this is a product of other things going on in their lives. It is not so much that they are in love with each other as that they are in love with the idea of being married, having their own home, and especially getting away from the family life in which they find themselves.

Teenagers who put themselves in the position of marrying early and even having a family often come to regret it. When the regrets and the problems in the marriage grow, there can be increasingly bad feelings and even possibly violent interaction. People tend to blame someone else for their own problems and to project their own failures onto others. It is easier to blame other people for your shortcomings than it is to accept the responsibility for them yourself.

Tom and Vicky are good examples of this situation.

Tom was the assistant manager of a drive-in theater. He called a psychiatrist for an appointment for evaluation and therapy. At his first session he told the doctor that he was there at the direction of a probation officer. The court had told him that he needed help. Tom was eighteen years old and had been arrested for assaulting his wife. She was seventeen and had filed a complaint after the police had been called one day when she and Tom had been in a violent exchange.

"It didn't start out this way," said Tom. "Vicky and I were really in love when we first met. We wanted to be together all the time. I couldn't stand to be away from her. I never would have dreamt that a year later I could be arrested for hitting her. I don't know what got into me. Maybe I'm crazy. It just seems to me that these things start to grow. The next thing I know she is teasing me or putting me down, or giving me a hard time, and I start to see red, and then I lose control. I push her and she hits me, and then we're off to the races."

Tom was reviewing some of the recent events that had led to his being required by the court to work out his family problems or go to jail. He chose the former, because he didn't want to be a jailbird. He didn't want to be away from his job, and he certainly didn't want to spend time locked up. The judge, after a hearing in which it became clear that Tom had actually knocked Vicky down several times and bruised her badly, felt that Tom had been out of control and definitely needed help.

"I guess the judge is right. He seemed to be a fair man. He wasn't trying to take sides. I did hurt Vicky, I guess, physically, I mean. She hurt me mentally, but I guess I hurt her the most. She was bruised, and I was really embarrassed when I saw her in court the next day. She's staying with her parents now. The judge said that we could get together and see each other if *you* said it was O.K. and she wasn't afraid anymore. Her lawyer said that you could talk to her, and maybe after you and the lawyer were satisfied, Vicky and I could work out some visits and try to get together again."

Tom and Vicky had met a year earlier at the drive-in. Vicky liked to go to the movies with her friends. One night she had trouble getting her car started after the show, and Tom came along and helped. He was able to fix the car without having to call a tow truck and thus saved Vicky a lot of money. They began to talk, and Tom offered to take her for a pizza. Her friends had left because they had to get up for school the next day. Vicky herself never cared much for school, and any excuse not to go was fine with her. Staying up late and having a pizza with Tom seemed like a great idea. She had never enjoyed an evening more. Tom was good-looking, and he was pleasant, and he was smart. He knew how to fix her car, and he had a job of his own, and he was only seventeen.

Tom had stopped going to school himself because he

didn't like it much either. His parents had agreed that he would be better off working. His relatives knew somebody in the movie chain who got him a job at the drive-in. Tom had been there for a few months and was doing very well. He had been promised that because of his performance and his honesty he would be promoted to manager in a year or so. He had a career ahead of him. He was the first person Vicky had met who was really independent.

Later Vicky recalled, when she too went for counseling, that she had never really been in the company of anybody who was independent. ''I was stuck with my mother all my life. She and my dad had divorced when I was only five or six years old. They had been fighting before that as far back as I can remember. My mom was afraid to be on her own, so she got married again only a few months after the divorce. That probably was the reason that they got the divorce in the first place. My dad had accused her of having a boyfriend, and I guess my stepfather was that guy. He's all right, I guess. He doesn't have much to do with me. When I was younger, I kept telling him to go away and leave me alone; I kept saying to him, 'You're not my dad.' After a while, I guess he believed it, and he never had much to say. My mom has been the one who has always tried to push me around and tell me what to do. She's the one who keeps saying that I'm not doing right. She kept telling me that my grades weren't good enough in school and that I'd never amount to anything. I knew I had to get out of there and always wanted to, but I didn't know how.

"When I met Tom, I figured he was my ticket out of

that house. He knew what to do and how to do things. He wasn't afraid. He was on his own and he had been for a year. His mom and dad had been divorced too. His mom, he said, had been an alcoholic. She was killed when he was only ten years old, in a car wreck. His father never married again, and Tom lived with his uncle and aunt. They were O.K., but they didn't care much about him. When Tom said he wanted to get out and be on his own and make his own way, they thought it was a good idea. His dad knew somebody to get him a job, and there he was, independent and making a living, and getting along, just like I always wanted."

As it turned out, Tom and Vicky began dating on a regular basis. Tom thought Vicky was pretty. Besides, she admired him, so he couldn't help but feel she had good taste. She hung on his every word and thought he was the smartest guy she had ever met. Maybe he was. It was certainly true that he was the only one she had ever met who was taking care of himself and and seemed to be getting ahead in life. She had never hung around with boys who had been very successful before. Most of them were in continuation school because they didn't do well in classes. A few were into drugs and dope, but Vicky never got much out of that. She thought they were going straight to reform school or jail and didn't feel comfortable with them. Tom didn't use dope or drugs, and he kept thinking about the future and how he was going to be a success.

Vicky's need to get away from home was probably the most important factor in what finally happened. She knew that if she and Tom kept seeing each other and getting more and more intimate, sooner or later she might get pregnant. She didn't try very hard *not* to get pregnant, because she wanted to be so close to Tom that she thought he might like it too. When it finally happened, she told him about it and was surprised that he wasn't as pleased as she was. She recalled his saying, "I thought you were taking care of that." He seemed to be angry and didn't want her to be pregnant or to have a baby. That surprised her a lot, and it hurt her too. She remembered telling him, "I thought you loved me and would want to have my baby so that we could have a baby together, a love baby."

"That's only in the movies, Vicky. I see enough of those things to know that it doesn't work out that way. I'm not ready to be a father and take care of a family. I've still got to get promoted to be the manager of some movie theater here in this town. That's not the kind of thing I want to do with a family. I love you and I like to be with you, but we're not ready to have kids yet."

Vicky reluctantly agreed that maybe he was right. She went ahead and had a therapeutic abortion. She was embarrassed by this, and never did tell her mom or stepdad about it. Her town had a family planning clinic, and she was able to go there and have the operation done in a doctor's office with a little suction machine. Tom paid the bill. They decided then that they would be much more careful.

Tom remembered thinking, "After that experience, I decided that Vicky and I had gone through a really strong emotional time. It wasn't easy telling her that I didn't want to have a baby with her then. I still wanted to have a baby with her, and I guess I still do. I just wasn't ready, and I didn't think we were, to do that kind of thing. That didn't mean that I didn't feel we should be together. I told her that I didn't believe in living together and not being married. I said that if she wanted to, we could get married. I just didn't feel we were ready for a family. That seemed to make her feel a lot better. She didn't seem to be as upset about the abortion when I told her that. I think I did the right thing. At least, I thought so at the time. Now, I'm not so sure.''

By the time they were married, Tom was just turning eighteen and Vicky was going to be seventeen. He didn't need anyone's consent or approval, but she had to go to her mother and stepfather. Although they didn't know about the abortion, they knew that Tom and Vicky had been very close. Because Vicky didn't seem to be interested in having much of a career, they thought getting married was the best thing she could possibly do. They encouraged it and even agreed to help pay for the wedding.

It was a small affair in a local church. The relatives all came, and although a lot of the older people felt that Tom and Vicky were ''too young to really be in love,'' they figured that the kids would learn as time went on ''if the marriage lasted.''

Tom and Vicky moved into a small apartment. Vicky got a job as an order taker and part-time waitress in the local fast-food restaurant. It only paid the minimum wage, but since she was ''an emancipated minor,'' she was happy with it. The money that she made was enough to pay the rent and a little bit of the expenses. Tom was able to take care of the rest with his salary, which was more than the minimum wage. He also received a percentage from the concessions at the drive-in, and was always working overtime to make more money. He had great ambition and drive and knew that someday he would become a special person, if he only stuck to it.

Vicky began to resent the fact that Tom was away every night. Of course, working in a drive-in theater means that you work only when it is dark. Tom had to be there at six o'clock at the latest. Sometimes, because he was the assistant manager, he had to close up and didn't get home until one or two in the morning. On weekends it was even later. He told Vicky that she could go with him some nights and stay in the office or watch the movie. But that didn't do her much good. She was tired because her job started early in the morning. She had the breakfast shift at the restaurant and was finished by two in the afternoon. They didn't get to see each other much except for a few hours in the early morning. Even their love life was not so good. Tom was tired from his long hours of work, and Vicky had to get up early while Tom was still asleep. The only times they had together were when she went over to the drive-in or in the late afternoon after she got home and before he left for work. It was at times like that that the arguments began. She was tired from work, and he was just awake. Sometimes he tried to make love to her, but she wasn't much in the mood for that and started to tease and needle him about it.

"Instead of the girl who kept telling me I was so smart and knew everything, and I was going to be a big success, I found that I was living with somebody who put me down as soon she walked through the door.'' Tom recalled that Vicky was in a foul mood when she came home from her job. She looked tired and washed out. She began to tell Tom, ''If you're such a big shot, how come your wife has to work taking orders in a crummy restaurant? I thought you were going to be a big shot in the movies. We've been married for six months now, and you don't make any more money than you did when we first got together. If it weren't for my job, we couldn't pay the rent on this place, big shot. I see guys who were in my class in high school who are doing better than you. Jackie's got a job at a gas station. He fixes cars and makes twice as much as you do, Mr. movie manager. And, of course, Francis is doing better than anybody. He's got himself a brand new Trans-Am and has nothing but money all day and all night long. Just because he pushes a little dope doesn't mean he's not a nice guy. I could have had him, you know. What am I doing here in this mousetrap of an apartment with an assistant manager who can't even afford more than a 1975 used Ford?''

Tom was really hurt by Vicky's put-downs and at first tried to reason with her. He pointed out that his job was just the first step and that persistence would get him ahead. Working as a mechanic in a gas station didn't have much future, he felt. And he wasn't interested in being a dope dealer and winding up dead on a slab in the morgue or in prison where he'd never see the light of day again. But Vicky wasn't really listening. She was just angry at not having the golden paradise that she had expected in her fantasies and dreams when they married.

"I guess one thing led to another," he recalled. "She began to tease me more and more. One day when she tried to show me a newspaper picture of a guy she knew winning a stock car race, I didn't want to pay attention to it. She poked the paper at me and pushed me. I don't know what happened then. As I told you before, I just saw red. I grabbed her arm and twisted it and told her, 'I don't want to look at your damn paper.' She hit me and I think I hit her again and again. I know I hit her two or three times, and she fell down. She began crying and screaming. I walked out and didn't come back till the next morning. I went straight to work; even though I got there two or three hours early, I had to get away to cool off.

"It wasn't much better the next day. She was still mad at me, and I was too embarrassed to talk about things."

That was just one of many confrontations that eventually led to the time when neighbors called the police. They were fighting so hard that things were being thrown and something went through a window. When the police arrived, Vicky was bruised and Tom's knuckles were scratched. Tom was arrested and spent the night in jail. He got a lawyer through his boss and was released the next day. Eventually, the judge put Tom on probation for assault and ordered that he get psychiatric treatment. It was suggested that Vicky receive treatment as well, and she too was placed in a family counseling center where she was able to talk about her feelings. Eventually, a family therapy situation was set up.

In the therapy it became clear that both Tom and Vicky had got married for the wrong reasons. Vicky wanted to get away from her family. Her stepfather valued her very little. Her father was absent and never seemed to want her. Her mother seemed to be uninterested, unconcerned, and just as unloving as everyone else. She looked around all of her teenage life for someone to love her. When she finally met Tom and he responded, she wanted only to live with him to get rid of her uncaring family.

Probably her motives were reasonable, but her approach was premature and excessive. The therapist pointed out to Vicky that there are other ways to have love. Lots of people can care for you and be interested in you and want to help you without involving marriage. Lots of girls have girlfriends who are warm and friendly and loving without any sexual contact. There are even relationships between boys and girls that have to do with friendship and warmth but without sexual activity. There is nothing wrong with boy-girl dating, and everyone needs to experience it as they go through high school and college. That doesn't mean, however, that every close relationship between a young man and young woman has to wind up at the altar. It's probably more accurate to say that people need to get to know each other very well before they even consider marriage. Usually teenagers go through several such relationships before they finally pick the person that they want to stay with for the indefinite future.

Vicky's need, then, was for love and closeness and to get away from her family, who, she felt, were restricting and controlling her. When she finally wound up in the marriage with Tom, it wasn't the kind of thing that met her every wish and fantasy and hope. Because of her disappointment and because she was angry at not having all of her dreams fulfilled, she began to berate Tom. She put him down for not satisfying her fantasies, not because he himself was inadequate. She teased and annoyed and harangued him until she aroused rage in him and even physical violence. Probably she even provoked the violence by poking him physically from time to time and challenging him to hurt her.

Tom, on the other hand, allowed himself to be provoked into rage to attack her. He was bigger and stronger and should have known better than to strike her. When Vicky started her needling, it was probably more appropriate for Tom to try to point out that she was overreacting and behaving in an immature and inappropriate way. If he wasn't able to do this himself, he should have sought out help. Because Tom didn't feel comfortable with other people, especially his aunt and uncle and his father, he didn't try to do that. He might have found that he could go to some of these older persons for counseling. His boss at the theater later turned out to be a very good friend. Had Tom gone to him in the first place, a lot of the trouble might have been avoided. The boss had told him that if he had known what was going on, he would have been able to offer some counseling himself. He had been through similar situations in the past and felt that he could have helped.

Other resources are available in a community when people need assistance, and the main thing is to know where they are and how to find them.

Tom's need to be independent and separate, his experience with a family in which the mother had died and there was no loving and close relative to take over, made it hard for him to see the need for help. His father was interested, but distant. His aunt and uncle did their duty but never really felt close to Tom, and he didn't feel close to them. He didn't believe he could go to anyone for guidance, and nothing could have been more destructive. There are lots of concerned people around, whether they be in church or school groups, in fraternal organizations, or even on the job, to whom one can turn for help. People generally turn out to be more good than bad; they are more likely to want to help than to harm. If you ask them for advice and assistance, they are flattered and enjoy giving it. Sometimes you need to ask more than one person for help in order to get the input of a number of ideas.

Of course, there are also professionals who can help. Family doctors, counselors, psychologists, even the psychologist of a school that you are no longer attending, can be called on. Young people who have established a good relationship with a school psychologist later still feel free to call on that person to talk about their difficulties and get advice or direction.

Tom and Vicky were able to get direction and guidance a little late, but still in time to save their marriage. The guidance and discussions, both at the counseling service and with the psychiatrist, helped both of them to see that their troubles, their anger and their fighting, were not related to anything wrong with the other person, but mainly within themselves. Once they were able to understand this and establish it in their minds, they started to get along better. The marriage was saved, and they were living together and making it. Tom had become a manager, and Vicky had been promoted too. She was now the assistant manager and was able to change her hours. Tom and Vicky had similar hours so that they had the same time off. They were able to do things together that were fun and worthwhile. They had a few more dollars in the bank. They were looking forward to more stability and eventually having a family when they were a little older.

As in the song we quoted at the beginning of the chapter, it may turn out that they were "not too young at all."

CHAPTER VII

Speed Kills

We all know that driving too fast on highways can result in death and destruction. The slogan ''Speed kills'' initially was used to warn against this kind of accident. In recent years, however, it has come to have another and equally ominous meaning. Speed, as most readers know, is a slang term for drugs that cause stimulation. These include a whole range of substances, starting with amphetamines and going on through cocaine. All of these drugs cause the user to feel ''up''; eventually, in higher doses, they can cause him to become confused, irritable, and agitated, and potentially to die.

There is no excuse for anyone ever to use illegal drugs. There is no reason for anyone to require the stimulation of outside chemicals. If one's life is not happy or productive or satisfying, there are much better ways to make it so than to take chemicals to induce an artificial feeling of well-being. Nevertheless, thousands and thousands of people, both young and old, use drugs and cause themselves and others to suffer the consequences.

Some few people, especially in their adolescent years, require stimulants for one reason or another. They don't know how to control them, and are not being given the medication appropriately by physicians. A disease called attention deficit disorder used to be known as minimal brain damage or, in some cases, hyperactivity. All three terms mean the same thing. They refer to an unusual situation, which affects about 5 percent of the population, in which medicines act paradoxically. A paradoxical reaction means that the medicine works opposite to the way we expect. Some people are stimulated by depressants such as phenobarbital, a tranquilizer. Others are calmed and tranquilized by stimulants such as the amphetamines or even the caffeine in coffee or tea.

These paradoxical reactions occur in persons whose brain has been injured, sometimes as early as birth or in the uterus before birth. Damage to the oxygen supply of the cerebrum, which is the part of the brain that does the thinking, can cause this disorder. It can be due to the fact that the delivery is difficult and the doctor has to use instruments, or that in some way the delivery is delayed or prolonged so that the baby's brain doesn't receive enough blood. In other instances the placenta, which is a part of the mother's body that is attached to the infant to supply blood, is not large enough and cannot adequately supply its needs. In still other cases the mother's use of drugs or substances of a toxic or poisonous nature during the pregnancy can cause the disorder. Accidents or injuries or infections that occur in the earliest years of life can cause the same damage.

As a result, the child becomes hyperactive, or unable to pay attention, or unable to read. These difficulties are all related to an injury to the brain tissue that doesn't show on X rays or brain scans but is evidenced in the behavior of the person. In these situations the use of small amounts of stimulants helps the person to focus attention, to learn, to read, and to do the other things that are difficult otherwise.

It was believed for many years that the use of medicines such as Ritalin, Cylert, and Dexedrine were useful in children from six to twelve but that then the child would "grow out of it." Nowadays, we understand that this does not always happen. A teenager may need *less* medicine than a growing child, but sometimes the need for the stimulant to reverse the effects of the birth trauma is still present. When that need is not met, or when the problem continues to exist, the person can become hyperactive, agitated, irritable, and even assaultive or violent.

If we understand what is going on with other members of our family, or sometimes schoolmates or friends, who have these kinds of problems, we can help them get the right kind of treatment to prevent continuing illness. Sometimes we can prevent tragic consequences. If the problem exists within ourselves and someone can point it out to us, we can seek assistance or get someone in the family to help us do so.

Godfrey C. had been diagnosed as "hyperactive" when he was a small child. At the age of eight, he had been restless and agitated in school for several years. He was always bright and clever and very verbal, but he never seemed to do well in class, and the teachers considered him "a troublemaker." It was only when Godfrey's condition was diagnosed as attention deficit disorder, which was then called hyperactivity, that he got any help. He was placed on small doses of Ritalin, which is a stimulant for most people, but which calmed him down and enabled him to think and focus and learn more effectively. Godfrey became a good student and got along well with his friends and even teachers. He was "transformed overnight" into an honor student and a credit to the school. He continued on the medication and continued to do well in school right through elementary school and into junior high. At that time, however, his family doctor and his mother especially decided that he didn't need so much medication. They gradually reduced the dosage. Godfrey seemed to get along well and had no trouble in school, with his friends, or in his conduct. By the time he was fourteen and ready to start high school, it was decided that he shouldn't be on any medication any longer.

That was fine with Godfrey, because he was embarrassed by having to take pills. He hated having to explain to his friends and peers why he had to do so. He sometimes sneaked the medicine at lunch time so nobody would notice he was taking it. He didn't want to appear to be different, or a freak.

Now in high school, he was even happier that he didn't have to take the pills, because he should have grown out of this childhood disease. He didn't want to be afflicted with something that bothered children. Godfrey wasn't going to be a nasty kid anymore, and he wasn't going to have trouble sitting still in class. He wasn't going to talk out of turn and throw spitballs and paper airplanes, and do all that other kid stuff. He knew better than that, and he certainly didn't need medicine to prove it.

And Godfrey was right. He didn't need to take medicine to avoid acting like a little kid, because he no longer was a little kid. He was a young man, an adolescent, and he knew better than to do the things he had done before. Unfortunately, however, the disease process, which had been initiated at his birth, continued. It was no longer likely that he would behave as he had when he was eight or nine years old, but there were other things that could cause trouble, and did.

After a year or so without Ritalin or similar medication, Godrey's brain did in fact become irritable again. He became short-tempered. He got into arguments and had no patience. From being friendly and having good relationships with the people around him, he found himself sneering at them and thinking them stupid. He looked down on them for not being as mentally quick as he was. He had no patience and didn't really care much about anyone.

As a result, he became more and more alienated from his old friends and started hanging out with the kids who used drugs. These kids are usually solitary in high school because they feel left out and unwanted. Godfrey didn't feel unwanted; he just didn't want to be bothered with too many other people. So he took up with the druggies, and he started using drugs once in a while. He knew he could handle it because he had taken Ritalin for so long. This time, however, he was using "crank," a street name for artificial stimulants such as amphetamines. At first, the crank didn't seem to affect him at all, probably because it calmed him down, just as the Ritalin did. Since it didn't affect him, he began to take more of it. He could take much more than the other kids without experiencing a rise or a high of any kind. Eventually, though, if he got enough of it into him, he could get just as high as the others, and sometimes even higher.

Godfrey liked to have his high and felt really good about it. He started looking more and more to the kids who dispensed the crank. Unfortunately, it became rather expensive. To support his growing need for the drug, he had to find a way to get it at less expense. The solution was to start selling it himself. When you sell, you keep a little back for your own use and thus don't get into financial difficulties.

Of course, it was only a temporary solution. As Godfrey used more and more, he had to get more and more money and increase his sales to support his growing habit. He didn't have much time for school anymore, and he found that he had to ditch twice as often to transact his business. By the time he was sixteen, he was an entrepreneur, but in illegal trafficking in drugs.

At first he only cut classes that he thought he could get away with. Eventually he was cutting them all. The school authorities initially didn't make much of it because Godfrey had been so smart and always was able to catch up. Finally his grades started falling seriously. The school counselors called the situation to the attention of his family but they were at a loss to explain what the problem really was. The family didn't understand it either.

Godfrey continued be truant, sometimes for days at a time. Sometimes he had to go out of town to get a larger supply of drugs. He was becoming a major dealer in his school. The business was getting increasingly dangerous, but Godfrey was caught up in it and didn't know how to get out. He was increasingly uncomfortable with the drug sales and afraid that he might get caught. Besides that, his own growing habit was beginning to scare him.

Godfrey was experiencing symptoms of drug toxicity. Amphetamines and stimulants in general can cause you to become very sick indeed. They have the effect of actually "burning out" your brain tissue. Overstimulation is like beating a sick horse to death: You begin to beat your brain for more and more energy by taking in more and more stimulants until your brain gives up entirely. Cases are on record of young people, and older people as well, becoming completely psychotic on stimulants. They lose control of their brain and act completely insane, which, in fact, they are.

Godfrey was getting hints of this kind of problem emerging. It scared him, but he wasn't sure how to get out of it.

Finally, fate got him out of it and into something much worse. While driving in a big hurry one day to get from one place to another—he never did remember from where to where—he was taking an awful lot of speed. Approaching the high school and going sixty or seventy miles an hour, he crashed into the car of a classmate who was coming around the corner at an average speed. Godfrey didn't see the other car as he careened around the corner, and of course the other driver didn't see Godfrey. The classmate was thrown out of the car and killed instantly. Curiously, Godfrey was hardly hurt at all physically. Mentally, he was shattered. He had killed somebody, and it had all happened because of the use of speed.

Godfrey was eventually charged with involuntary manslaughter, as the result of plea bargaining between his family's lawyer and the district attorney's office. It was too late to bring back the young man who had been killed in the crash, but possibly there was time to save Godfrey. The authorities ordered Godfrey placed in an institution where his use of drugs could be controlled and where it could be better determined what had been going wrong with him in the two years before the accident.

As Godfrey's case was gradually unraveled in the institution, it became clear that he had been agitated for several years. Somewhere along the line, someone might have been able to prevent the tragedy. When it became apparent that Godfrey was no longer hanging out with his old friends, someone might have said something. When it became obvious that Godfrey was increasingly irritable, angry, and short-tempered, that would have been a good time for intervention. When Godfrey started to get into fights with his classmates and actually became violent with other people, that might have been a time for someone to take some action.

It is unfortunate that hindsight is always 20/20. It's easy to look back and see where you should have taken action after a tragedy has occurred. It's easy for a doctor to look over the history of a patient and say, "Why didn't you do something back then?" or "Why didn't your mother or father,'' or "Why didn't your sister or brother,'' or "Why didn't your friends try to intervene?'' No one can be perfect. It is important, however, for us all to be alert.

In looking back at the events that led to this great tragedy and his overwhelming guilt, Godfrey pointed out, "I never started out any day being mad at anybody. I never started out any day being angry or trying to get into a fight. I was never a bully or someone who wanted to hurt other people. It's just that I found myself getting more and more angry. I started taking the speed because it did make me feel good. Maybe I never should have stopped taking the Ritalin in the first place. I don't know; that's not for me to say. All I know is that when I started buying the crank from one of my friends, I liked it more and more. The more I took, the more I felt happy. It was almost as if I needed it every day and more than once a day. I did notice that I was getting nasty and angry and that I was looking down my nose at people. Now when I look back, I realize I was wrong. If only we could turn back the clock, the whole world would be different.''

Godfrey was very sad as he reviewed the history of his increasing abuse of amphetamines and stimulants and his inability to control it. In the institution he had had a lot of time to think things through. He was filled with remorse and regret. He realized that he had been the instrument of a violent death, and he thought he would never get over the tragedy. That is probably true.

An important part of working with people is to help them understand how they got where they are and how they can avoid its happening again. Another very important dimension of the work is to help other people to avoid making the same mistakes. "If I could prevent one other person from getting into the tragedy that I got into, that might make up for it," said Godfrey. It was his plan when he was released to join some groups. He wanted to go into the community and tell others about his experience. He believed that if he could get his message across, he might prevent others from having the same kind of tragedy.

Godfrey stayed in the institution for about a year and a half while he worked out some of his feelings. He was again put on small doses of Ritalin, because he still had the attention deficit disorder. He had only got into stimulants and amphetamines in an attempt at self-medication. Treating yourself means that you have a fool for a doctor and a fool for a patient.

The real lesson to be learned from Godfrey's case is that there are a number of people, in junior high school and high school and even in college, who abuse substances such as cocaine and amphetamines. Some may have diseases. Some may be hyperactive people who were never diagnosed as children. Others may be hyperactives who were thought to have grown out of it but never really did. Others may just want "to get high" and are abusing substances for some psychological reason.

In any of these cases, another person may be able to help. If that other person is a friend, he or she can speak about it. One of the most positive things you can do to help a friend is to point out how things really are.

There is nothing wrong with telling the truth, even if you think that it's not going to make your friend feel good. If your friend realizes that you are genuine in your efforts to help, he or she will even allow you to be wrong sometimes. It is better to talk about a problem than to walk away from it or hide it. If you have a friend who you think is irritable, angry, jumpy, and having trouble learning in school, it might be worthwhile to talk to him or her about it. Maybe he needs to consult a psychologist or an educational expert to see if there is some reason why he is not learning well. Maybe he needs to go to the family doctor to find out why he is acting different.

If you know that someone is using stimulants or speed or cocaine, it's important to confront him or her with the fact and point out how dangerous it can be. You are not being a ''stool pigeon'' to talk to your friend about how he is hurting himself. A good friend is able to tell both the good and the bad. A person who can listen to friends and respect what they have to say, even if it is unpleasant, is really a good friend. One doesn't find too many close friends in the world. If you have one and you value him or her, it's worthwhile to talk to him. If Godfrey had had someone to talk to him about what was happening, possibly the tragedy could have been avoided.

The smartest thing that anyone can do is to know when to seek an expert and where to find him. If you have a problem, you should seek help from someone who knows how to deal with it. If you don't even know that you have a problem, it's up to a friend who can see it more objectively to point it out.

The use and abuse of all kinds of substances is increasing in our society. Often it starts in junior high school, high school, and college. These institutions are the places where the future of our country begins. It is important for all of us to work together to halt the ever-growing contagion of drug abuse. When there is a real reason for someone to use a drug, in which case we call it medication, it is important to discover that and to deal with it effectively. Medication has a real purpose in life, which is to alleviate pain and to cure people. Used otherwise, we find ourselves in an ever escalating situation in which the frightening phrase "Speed kills" is all too true.

CHAPTER VIII

*"I Could **Kill** Them!"*

The biblical injunction "Honor thy father and mother" is frequently disobeyed both emotionally and mentally. Unfortunately, the same thing occurs when physical violence is directed against parents. It is relatively unsurprising these days to read stories in the newspapers about parents who abuse their small children, but it is rare that one reads or hears about young people attacking their parents.

There *are* cases in which adolescents have assaulted their parents. Such incidents can be avoided if the situation is understood. Sometimes the problem is the mental illness of a child, who has a distorted understanding of what's going on around him or what is driven mad by internal demons that have nothing to do with the relationship with the parents. In other cases, however, there is a specific reason. If one can understand the situation and intervene before violence has occurred, it can be avoided.

Even people who are, in fact, mentally ill and capable of violence against their parents can be treated before the illness reaches overwhelming proportions. They can be helped before the acting out of rage and the resulting punishment and guilt, which can ruin their lives. Lots of people say, "I could kill them," and don't really mean it. But even saying it is something we must take seriously.

Malcolm P. was a seventeen-year-old high school student who began to feel rage toward both his father and his mother when they began to bicker and argue. Eventually, the marriage was so filled with hate and anger that the parents did the adult thing for once in their lives and were divorced. Malcolm was so enraged at this disruption of his secure home that he became increasingly angry and considered violence.

Initially, his hate was directed against his father, who he felt had deserted the mother. He then began to imagine that his father was secretly trying to control him through radio broadcasts, television signals, and messages in code in the newspapers. Later, he began to believe that he had telepathic communication with people from other countries and from around the United States who were telling him how to live his life and what to do from moment to moment because of the influence of his hated father.

When his mother tried to intervene and point out to him that these were imaginary voices and imaginary communications, Malcolm became angry with her too. Ultimately, when he began to answer the voices and respond aloud to the television communications, his mother became alarmed and sought psychiatric help. in the meantime, however, Malcolm became increasingly angry with her and threatened to strike her when she interfered with his ideas, thoughts, and plans.

It became clear to the doctor that the situation was potentially dangerous, and when Malcolm seemed about to attack his mother in the doctor's office, he had to be physically restrained. Since he was a rather large fellow, it was necessary to call the police, and ultimately Malcolm had to be hospitalized. Later, he was given medication that calmed him down, and he became able to listen to the voices of reason instead of those inside his frightened mind. He slowly began to understand that the divorce of his parents was in no way related to him or to anything that he had done. He had been carrying around a great deal of guilt and self-hate because, in some way, he felt he was responsible for the divorce and for the rupture of his home and the safety and warmth that he had known since infancy.

Malcolm P. was not an unusual case in a psychiatrist's office. A great many young people experience guilt and self-hate but don't openly reveal it. They feel useless and flawed and inadequate but hold it tightly within themselves, and sometimes it is up to friends, relatives, and others to be of help. Young people who seem to be confused or agitated need the help of their friends. When you know that someone who is in your class or is close to you as a friend is experiencing the trauma of parental marital problems or financial difficulties, you can help by being a friend. Sometimes it is important to talk to him or her and suggest seeking professional help. Many people are ashamed or embarrassed to seek pyschiatric, psychological, or other mental health resources. Because of this, the support and encouragement of comrades is important.

Early diagnosis of problems such as those of Malcolm can help to prevent the illness from getting worse. Most of these illnesses can be improved significantly if they are caught early and the right treatment is begun. Malcolm could have been placed on medication and enabled to talk to people who understood these matters much earlier than he was. As a result, many of the embarrassing, frightening, and distressing things that he experienced could have been avoided.

As it was, long-term treatment was instituted for him. In addition, his parents consulted a counselor so that they could better understand him and how to deal with him. Malcolm lived in a treatment center for a while and went to school at the same time. While there he began to understand himself and the problems that he was experiencing. Ultimately, he was able to return to his regular high school and graduate with his class. It was important during this period of time that his classmates understand and deal with him as they would anyone else who had an illness, went away, got better, and returned to the mainstream of life.

It was necessary for Malcolm to remain on medication for an extended period to avoid future episodes of confusion and fear and even violence. It enabled him to continue with his life, to graduate from high school, and to avoid further trouble with his family, himself, and those around him.

Shari B. was a fourteen-year-old high school freshman who was having increasing trouble controlling her feelings. Shari was the only child of concerned and interested parents who didn't always know how to deal with her. Her father was a professional man who traveled most of the week. He tried to come home on weekends but couldn't always do so. Shari's mother kept the home and also had a part-time job in town.

Shari felt that her parents were not much interested in her, and she began to believe that was because there was something wrong with her. She was afraid she wasn't interesting, worthwhile, bright enough to attract wholesome friends or to be with the "in crowd." As a result, she began hanging out with other people who felt that they were left out too. Because these people felt that others didn't like them, they tried to act in ways consistent with lack of acceptance. They were the ones who used drugs, drank alcohol, and got into a variety of activities that society frowned upon. Shari began by smoking marijuana, which her new friends provided. She tried various kinds of pills that were offered to her, reds and whites and a whole variety of colors. They attracted her, even though they didn't do much to make her feel better. She also began to drink alcohol, hoping to be more acceptable to her new buddies. Eventually, of course, she got no better feeling from any of these substances; but she thought that if she used them at home her parents might notice and pay more attention to her. Shari later said,

"Nobody cared about me, and nobody paid much attention to me. They weren't interested in how I felt, just what I did. They wanted me to get good grades in school and to be accepted by all 'the right people.' They wanted me to belong to the cheerleading squad. They wanted me to be an athlete. They wanted me to be in the Honor Society. They never asked me very much about what *I* wanted, and they didn't seem to care. My new friends didn't want anything from me but to be my friend. So what, if they used drugs. They had a right to do that. After all, most of their parents drank, and some of them probably used drugs too. You probably use drugs yourself, Doctor, don't you? Well, most adults do, only they deny it.''

Shari was very angry and bitter toward the entire adult society. Mainly it was focused on her parents because of her belief that they didn't care about her. She began to act in more and more upsetting ways at home. At first they assumed that her behavior was only part of her growing up, but eventually they became alarmed. They didn't know what to do to control her, her behavior, or her use of illegal drugs. At the same time, they told each other that it was probably all right because they had read that using marijuana or cocaine wasn't physically harmful to people. Even though that is wrong, it's the kind of belief that people like to have because it relieves them from having to do anything drastic or dramatic. Most people have difficulty doing the right thing because it requires the expenditure of a lot of energy, causes others to disagree with them, and creates conflict.

Whatever the reason, Shari's parents didn't prevent her from using drugs, and eventually she went further and further. In one way Shari thought that she could probably get away with anything because her parents didn't care. At the same time, however, she wanted to see how far she could go. ''I knew my parents didn't give a damn about me. They let me smoke pot in the house, and they let me take pills. They said they did that because they knew I would grow out of it. What it really meant was that they didn't care what I did and never had cared. Generally speaking, I got the feeling that I could do almost anything and they wouldn't say a word. I wanted to see how far I could go. I guess I really wanted to have them care about me and pay attention. But it never came out that way.''

Shari became increasingly uncomfortable because she seemed to be getting away with more and more. Finally, she felt that she had to test the limits as far as she could. Most doctors and psychologists know that people need to have limits in their lives. Young people need to feel that their parents know things and are in control. Because they are too young to understand everything about the world, they want to believe that their parents are wise enough and thoughtful enough to help them in dealing with the problems of life. They need limits even though they don't want to be controlled and pushed around. Shari had this kind of feeling and began to test to see how far the limits would go.

She began to do more and more outrageous things in an effort to get help. That may seem strange, but when people need help they often ask for it in ways other than using the words, ''Help me.'' They act in a way that will attract attention and finally get someone else to say, ''Do you need help from me?'' Shari tried by challenging her parents, especially her mother, to try to control her.

Because Shari was growing so fast and actually was almost the size of her mother, her mother had stopped attempting to discipline her physically and had turned the job over to the father. Since he was away so much, Shari knew that she could get away with almost anything. She knew that she could control her mother physically, and her mother was becoming afraid of her. Finally, Shari threatened to strike her mother when she didn't do what Shari wanted. Her mother was embarrassed and intimidated by this and kept quiet about it, not even telling her husband. She found herself in a position in which her fourteen-year-old daughter was disciplining her as if she were the child.

Eventually, however, she confessed to her husband that Shari had actually hit her on one occasion and that she felt powerless to prevent it. Since Shari's father was a bright man and professionally oriented, he recognized the need to get outside help in a situation that had got so far out of control that the roles were reversed between the mother and daughter.

Shari's father consulted with the family physician. The family doctor is frequently the best informed person to talk to in situations of family stress. He has a good understanding of the various members of the family, usually having known them for some years. He is aware of their strengths and weaknesses and as an informed yet objective observer can often make suggestions that family members themselves are unable to make.

The family doctor usually is informed concerning the resources available in the community. When a specific specialist is needed, he knows who it is and who would best match the needs of a particular family. In this case, the father explained to the doctor that Shari and her mother were in conflict and that he was unable to control the situation because of his frequent absences. In addition, he said that his wife was intimidated by her daughter and, at the same time, Shari herself was frightened at her power and was like a car racing downhill without any brakes.

The family doctor suggested that a trained family counselor would be helpful. The community had a family counseling center whose staff included trained clinical social workers, psychologists, and others with mental health training. Many such centers have a psychiatrist on call in case there is a need for medication or more intensive treatment. The family doctor arranged an appointment for Shari and her mother at the family counseling center. Later, the father went along to give the therapist his view of the situation.

Eventually, it was decided that the family would be most adequately served by counseling as a family group. Shari's dad arranged his work schedule so that he could keep Monday appointments and go about his business for the rest of the week. He became a participant in the therapy, which was a big positive step for all of them. It gave his wife some backup and security, and it enabled Shari to feel that she was not like a runaway car. The father had always been a figure of strength and resourcefulness in the family, and so he proved to be in this situation.

As counseling went on, Shari's mother came to understand that controlling her child was not part of discipline or punitive measures. It wasn't corporal punishment or vindictiveness, but a necessary role for a parent to play in helping a young person to grow up and become mature. The father learned that it was important for him to be an integral part of the family, not a disinterested observer who comes in from time to time to see how things are going. The father is part of the whole family and its activities and needs to participate. Shari herself was taught that rebelling and exploding only made her feel more insecure and more out of control. She began to understand that self-control and self-discipline are part of growing up and that she could learn to like herself better under those circumstances.

The therapist tried to remain a sounding board for the entire group. At the same time, she tried to instill the realization that the family had to continue the treatment even when things started to go better at the beginning. She insisted that frequent visits were necessary. Even if it seemed a sacrifice on the part of the father because of his job, and on the others because of their other interests, it was well worth it. Each member of the family felt that the others were contributing and taking the time and trouble to be involved in solving a major family problem.

Because of this, Shari began to feel more worthwhile and more important within her family. That helped her to feel that she was worthwhile elsewhere as well and might amount to something in the long run.

After a year or so of group therapy, it was clear that the family had, in fact, pulled themselves together. Shari continued to see the therapist for some time after her parents were no longer involved. She needed other help to understand herself, her intimate and personal feelings about herself and her peers. It became important for her to learn to relate to other teenagers of both sexes, not just as "the bad one," to see herself as a valuable member of the school and the community, not just an onlooker or an excluded "also ran." She *did* begin to develop this kind of feeling. Her grades improved, and she applied to college with the hope that going on to a new environment with a fresh start would hold even more promise for a positive and constructive future.

CHAPTER IX

Sexual Violence

It is now almost a hundred years since Sigmund Freud, the father of psychoanalysis, began writing about childhood sexuality. His theories created a storm of protest in Victorian Vienna. Freud was not even heard at the Academy of Medicine meetings when he started to talk about children having sexual fantasies and experiences: Most of the members of that august body walked out on him.

His problem was that he was talking about a major taboo, and the fact that he later began to discuss children's thoughts about incest was even worse. That was and always has been a taboo of the first order. The thought that adults would even consider having sexual intercourse or sexual play with children is totally unthinkable in all societies, with rare exceptions. Except for the bizarre practice of the royal families of Egypt of marriage between brothers and sisters, such behavior is prohibited in every culture that anthropologists have studied. The Egyptians believed that their royal families were gods and that a god could mate only with another god. Thus incest was inevitable.

The reason that incest is taboo in human society is very simple and biologically sound. The basis of human reproduction is genetic linking and cross-linking to make a different individual. When people from the same family intermarry, their genes are too similar and genetic faults are reproduced. Such genetic faults have been known even in mating of first cousins; hence some of the major bleeding problems found in the royal families of Europe. When close relatives mate and reproduce, the recessive genes for faulty characteristics, such as hemophilia, some forms of brain disease, epilepsy, and other hereditary diseases, are reproduced. That makes them, instead of recessive, a dominant characteristic of the child. The trait is then reproduced over and over in each generation.

Societies for thousands of years have recognized this effect, even though they didn't understand the scientific basis for the flaws. They therefore prohibited the mating of brothers and sisters, parents and children, and even first cousins. Such a prohibition is called in primitive tribes a "taboo." Essentially, it is the same in modern society, which prohibits marriage between first cousins and brothers and sisters.

When Freud first heard stories of incest from his patients, he was shocked. They were so frequent and the thoughts about them were so vivid and startling that he was at a loss to understand them. After all, he himself was a product of nineteenth-century middle-class society, which denounced and prohibited such matters and actually made their discussion unacceptable. He finally decided that the incestuous stories of his patients were not true, but were actually only fantasies. That ultimately led to his theory of the Oedipus complex. It was based on the Greek play by Sophocles in which Prince Oedipus unwittingly murders his father and later marries his mother and lives with her as king.

Freud considered this play symbolic in nature, representing the wish of every young boy to destroy his father, to possess his mother sexually, and to have her stay with him as her favorite child. Freud extended the Oedipal fantasy to suggest that it existed in every child's fantasy life and was part and parcel of the growing-up process. The theory became the cornerstone of Freudian psychoanalytic treatment. The idea was to grow out of this feeling, identify with the father as a positive figure, and "if you can't lick him, join him." Thus, the young boy would become more like his father and when he grew up would find another woman to marry.

The notion that children actually acted out incestuous thoughts with their own parents or other adults was, in Freud's mind, unacceptable. He considered it too common a fantasy. When his patients told him that it had happened to them, he tended to discount it. Only in recent years have we become aware that he probably was wrong. The problem is far more common (to some extent epidemic in nature) than has ever been imagined. With the reporting of physical child abuse becoming more and more frequent, mental health workers, psychologists, and psychiatrists have come to realize that another kind of abuse is going on. That is the sexual abuse of children. It often takes the form of incestuous activity, and it is one of the most violent things described in this book.

It is probably true that the kind of sexual abuse and incestuous activity that goes on now is not new. It seems likely that it was just as common if not more so fifty and a hundred years ago, but it was not reported. Incest can have grave and extremely destructive consequences to the growing child and can create feelings of guilt and inadequacy in the adult perpetrator as well.

Many women who were molested as children become either totally frigid or unresponsive sexually. They can develop a number of psychosomatic symptoms, including migraine headaches, ulcers, colitis, and painful menstrual problems.

A common result of childhood molestation in the adult woman is that although she becomes able to have intercourse with an adult man, either in or out of marriage, she is unable to be sexually free. She feels generally uncomfortable during the entire sex act and may not be able to achieve orgasm. Often, this unresponsiveness is hidden from her awareness, and she doesn't even report it as a symptom. Later, when she learns through reading or talking with friends that she is not experiencing orgasm, she is baffled as to the origin of the problem and never connects it with her early sexual experiences. That is because such events are so distressing to children that they are totally repressed from memory; the memory is actually not available to their conscious awareness as adults. Professional treament is sometimes the only way to uncover the root of the problem. Some case examples will illustrate this more dramatically.

Mary B. was a thirty-five-year-old, unmarried private secretary who sought treatment initially because of chronic migraine headaches that were causing her extreme distress and time lost at work. She had a responsible job for an important executive and could not afford to miss time at work. She sometimes went to the office under great pressure with a headache that almost incapacitated her. She recognized that the problem was likely to interfere with her career, and she was dependent on her job for her livelihood and the life-style that it afforded her.

After several months of psychotherapy, Mary's headaches persisted. Finally, the analysis began to delve into her early life, and in one session she recalled an episode that had occurred when she was twelve years old. A devout Roman Catholic, she recalled a feast day when she had been assigned to be in a pageant at the church. She remembered that she had gone with the priest into the basement to get some materials that were stored there. She related that the priest had begun to touch her and eventually had molested her in a sexual manner. During the course of the session, she cried copiously and hysterically. At the end of the hour the doctor told Mary that the recollection was very important and would be useful in helping her to deal with her problems. She seemed to understand and agreed to discuss it further on her next visit.

When Mary returned the following week, she reported that she had had no headaches at all since the previous visit and was delighted with the turn of events. When the doctor told her that this was very likely to be related to the revelations of the previous week concerning her childhood, she flatly denied ever having had such an experience. She denied having reported it and clearly had repressed the entire matter.

Eventually, she and the doctor were able to work through the problem and get the material out on the surface so that she could understand it. The experience certainly had a great deal to do with her never marrying and never having any sexual activity. Eventually, she was able to establish more appropriate relations with the opposite sex, and although she did not marry, she was at least able to have a normal sexual life.

With the advent of more and more family counseling centers and mental health clinics in the United States, a greater amount of material is being uncovered concerning sexual abuse of children. It has been known for many years that men and women who were physically abused when they were children repeat the behavior when they marry and have their own families; that is, they begin abusing their own kids. It is now becoming clear that the same thing holds true for children who were abused sexually as youngsters. When they grow up, they often slip into the pattern of abusing their own children, or at least allowing the abuse to occur by marrying someone with a similar background and experience and then not doing anything to prevent the spouse from acting in a sexual manner toward the children.

Sexual abuse can start as early as six or seven years old, but similar situations arise with adolescents and teenagers. Often the sexual misbehavior on the part of the parent doesn't begin until the child is reaching puberty, sometimes at eleven, twelve, or thirteen. It is then that the problem begins to show itself and then that something must be done. Unfortunately, these problems are not discovered until many years later unless the family, the young person affected, or some other person close to the situation is aware of what is going on and its implications and also has the courage to report it to the appropriate authorities.

A good example of this kind of problem was the case of Joan A. Joan was twenty-five years old when she began having difficulties in her family life. She went to a marriage counseling service and was seen by the counselors and also by the psychiatrist in consultation because of the constant fighting between her and her husband. The friction was beginning to affect their two young children, and they were afraid it would destroy the children's lives as well as their own marriage.

In the course of taking a careful history of Joan, it was revealed that she had been sexually molested by her stepfather. She wasn't sure exactly when it had begun, but she reported, "He began coming around and touching me and teaching me about sex, he said, when I started to have my periods. I don't remember if I was twelve or thirteen. All I remember is feeling embarrassed and ashamed and very, very scared." She said that her stepfather had been married to her mother for three or four years at the time. He was a minister, and her mother had married him because she thought he would be a virtuous and hard-working man who would take care of her and her children and teach the children the right ways of life.

"He taught me, all right. He taught me all about sex; at least, that's what he said. He told me that he didn't want me to learn in the wrong way. He said he wanted me to stay away from street people and drugs and alcohol, so he was going to teach me everything I needed to know about sex. He started by teaching me how to 'French kiss.' He would put his tongue into my mouth, and I felt terrible about that. But my mother didn't seem to mind. She didn't interfere, and when I finally told her that I felt Daddy Paul was being too 'close' in his lessons to me, she laughed it off.''

Joan was, as many young people are, embarrassed and frightened by the sexual contact. Even though she had the courage to talk about it with her mother, which is very unusual, nothing was done. That is one of the unfortunate problems that arise more and more often in our awareness of child abuse: Sometimes the mother is so embarrassed by her husband's behavior that she doesn't want to believe it's happening. If a child hints around that something wrong is going on, the mother often tries to laugh it off, minimize it, or act as if it didn't happen at all.

By the time Joan was fifteen, she began to feel more and more angry and tried again to tell her mother specifically how ''Daddy Paul'' was acting toward her.

''I told my mother that Daddy Paul was beginning to touch me on my breasts and in my private parts. I told her exactly what he was doing and that he said it was 'for my own good.' My mother didn't believe me. She said that I had too active an imagination and that *she* never saw it anyway. She said that I had been talking like this for a couple of years and obviously no harm had come to me, so she couldn't believe that anything wrong was going on. She made me feel as if I were the one who was bad. She made me feel dirty, and she made me feel ashamed. She made me think that maybe I was making it up and that there was something wrong with me and not with her husband. I decided to stop talking to her about it altogether. I was too ashamed to talk to anybody else about it, and you're the first person that I have told in ten years.''

Her mother really wouldn't listen. She didn't want to believe what Joan was saying; she felt too threatened by the notion that her husband might, in some way, be unfaithful to her or be an evil, incestuous, and villainous person. The best way to handle this, in the mother's mind, was to deny it totally. While doing that, of course, she also created a terrible guilt situation for Joan, which persisted to the day that she began treatment and for some time afterward. It is much easier to create guilt than to remove it.

There are thousands of cases like this all over the world. The real problem is not understanding how they come about, but correcting them. It wasn't until Joan was twenty-five years old that she would talk openly and seriously about her problem.

The therapist suggested that Joan's mother, who lived in a nearby town, be asked to come in and participate in a family therapy session. Reached on the telephone, the mother couldn't understand why anybody would want to talk with her. When she was told, however, that her daughter's marriage was at stake, as well as the welfare of her grandchildren, she reluctantly agreed to come in, "but only for one time." Clearly, she felt threatened by the situation and obviously, too, at some level of her consciousness she was aware that something was going on in the background. It might have to do with the stories that Joan had told her in the past, and she simply did not want to confront them nor deal with them in any serious manner.

When the mother finally came to the therapist's office, she completely denied the story, saying again that her daughter had imagined it and that her husband could not possibly be involved in any such activity. Joan suggested that his proclivity might possibly be the reason that the husband's first marriage had ended in divorce and that his first family had not spoken to him for more than twenty years, but her mother simply would not face the problem.

"There you go again, Joan. You're always imagining things. I am sure that Paul has a very good reason for not seeing his first family. I know it couldn't possibly have to do with anything as absurd as sexual misconduct. After all, Paul is a minister. He has a high standing in the community and the church. No one would ever dream of accusing him of anything like this but you. It's probably some of your same childhood imagination."

When the doctor said he believed that Joan's memory might very well be correct and that it was not uncommon for this kind of problem to surface, the mother retorted defensively:

"Well, that may be your experience, Doctor, and that may be the kind of people that you see in this clinic and in these offices, but it's not what we're used to where I come from. We don't have that kind of people in our town, and if we did they wouldn't stay very long. I'm afraid that Joan has taken you in, perhaps because it's the kind of thing you want to hear in your business. In our family, we don't want to hear that kind of thing, and we don't believe those stories."

One of the major problems encountered in dealing with this kind of misconduct is the possibility, and in many cases the probability, that the parent of the opposite sex will not believe the accusation. This is especially distressing for children of six, seven, and eight. Adults rarely believe such an accusation made by small children, yet psychological testing over the years reveals that children are not capable of creating the kind of sexual fantasies that these accusations would require. It is not within the scope of a child's imagination to create sexual activities involving adult genitalia, their uses and activities, unless they have experienced or witnessed them. Nevertheless, parents are very anxious not to believe what is being said, and that creates a great trauma to the child.

The same is true of young adolescents or even teenagers, but at least they have other resources. They have access to people who will listen. Most young people have contact with school counselors and teachers. Sometimes there is one teacher with whom you feel close and can talk openly. If you are on an athletic team, the coach may be the person closest to you. In other situations, relatives such as grandparents, aunts, and uncles can be approached or a neighbor can listen and be sympathetic and understanding. It isn't just the parent who can be talked to. This kind of issue is not "a one-shot deal"; that is, if you talk to someone and don't get a reasonable response, it is not inappropriate to find someone else to contact. Sexual abuse is a major problem that requires significant thought and energy, and that can have long-term repercussions.

In Joan's case it was very important that she was able, even at twenty-five, to make a breakthrough and talk about her problem. She was able to deal with the fact that not only did these things actually happen, but that her mother needed to deny it. At first she could not understand why her mother needed to make this denial and somehow felt that she herself was responsible for everything. Finally Joan was able to grasp how terrified her mother was of realizing the truth. If the mother's husband were to lose his position in the community, she, too, would be downfallen. She, too, would be removed from a position of respect. Not only that, she would have to leave him or at least have a strained relationship with him. After having had one failed marriage, she was in no way able to tolerate facing another in the offing.

Joan finally was able to see why this was so, and even though she didn't like it, she was in a position to deal with it and try to work through the problems. Able now to perceive the damage that had been done in her life by her stepfather, she was able to begin to examine her own feelings about men and her relationships with them.

The revelation did, in fact, allow her marriage to become more successful. Initially it wasn't clear that she was able to have great sexual satisfaction, but at least she had stopped bickering and fighting with her husband. The marriage was smoother and less explosive, which would have a positive effect on the children. If both partners kept working at it, they might, in the long run, achieve a more successful resolution of the sexual problem as well.

Sometimes instead of inhibiting the ability to accept sexual activity in marriage, childhood experiences of molestation can cause the opposite kind of problem. A young person, especially a girl, who has experienced sexual molestation in puberty or even younger begins to feel useless, dirty, and guilty and that the sexual activity was her own fault. That is the "magical thinking" of children in which everything that happens to them is caused by their own acts, thoughts, or wishes. They come to believe that because they think about something, it actually comes true. This "magical thinking" is not unusual in children; the real problem is that it is not true. Because of it, many children who become involved in an incestuous or other sexual situation, which is always initiated by an adult, feel that it is their own fault.

Wendy B. was a seventeen-year-old who was seen in a family counseling center because of problems of a sexual nature. Wendy had been sent by a judge for counseling because she had been expelled from school and kept getting picked up by police vice officers. She was found to have become sexually promiscuous and was called a menace to the community.

Wendy was extremely reluctant to talk to the therapist, and felt that it was silly for the judge to have ordered it. "I guess it's the kind of thing that judges have to do, Doc, don't they?" Wendy was trying to suggest that if both she and the therapist treated the session as a kind of necessary evil, it would lessen the pain for both sides. She wanted to make the therapist feel that they were just going through the motions. As soon as a letter could be sent to the judge saying that Wendy had appeared, the whole matter could be dismissed, and everyone would be happy. She even suggested, "Why don't you just say that I was here and send a letter to the judge after a few months to tell him that. That way, we can all be happy. You can get paid for my visits and not have to do any work. I won't have to waste time doing this kind of thing, so I'll be happy. The judge will be happy because he'll think we did what he said."

When the therapist rejected this rather cynical suggestion, Wendy seemed surprised that anyone didn't want to take advantage of a situation in which they could be paid for doing nothing. She herself considered it an ideal way to deal with life. The concept of getting satisfaction and enjoyment out of doing a job was one she had never seriously considered.

It finally became clear to Wendy that she would have to enter into the treatment relationship, but she did so reluctantly. It took many months of regular visits to get her to reveal some of the experiences she had as a child. At the age of twelve, which is late for this kind of thing to happen, she was molested by her father.

Wendy had come home from school early because she was ill. Her father was in bed, drunk and apparently half asleep. When he saw her, however, he asked her to bring him a cup of coffee. Wendy was pleased to do it, because she loved her dad and felt that he cared about her too, despite the fact that "maybe he drank a little too much." She made the coffee and took it to him, and he asked her to sit down on the bed and help him drink it. He was still apparently intoxicated, but Wendy understood that and tried to hold the cup for him and help him to drink. The next thing she knew ''he was putting his hand on my legs. He started this kind of creeping thing up my leg, and at first I hoped it was just an accident. I thought maybe he just put his hand there by accident, but it wasn't. He did it on purpose. He knew what he was doing, and he kept doing it. Finally, he began to grab and squeeze my keester.''

Wendy began to sob and became extremely upset during the discussion of this event. It had taken her many months to get to the point of revealing it, and it was extremely painful for her.

''He wanted to do it. He was trying to squeeze my ass. He liked the idea of touching me between the legs. He was getting hard. I could see it. I knew it was something that I had done. It was my fault. I should never have sat on the bed with him. I should never have have put my hand behind his neck and tried to help him drink the coffee. He thought I was trying to make love to him. I know. I've seen it happen a lot of times since then. I'm only seventeen, but I've been with an awful lot of guys. It doesn't take a lot sometimes to turn them on. I did it to my dad, and I could do it to anybody. I could do it to you too, Doctor, if you'd let me.'' She was by now very upset, crying as she talked and sobbing deep, painful sobs. She was filled with guilt and sure that somehow it was entirely her fault that her father had been led to this degradation—a degradation that she felt she had deserved. She was unable to understand that it was the adult who was responsible, that it is always the adult's responsibility in such situations to act in an adult manner.

One can't expect a child to be an adult by the very definition of the terms. Children are not responsible for sexual activities between themselves and a parent, even though they feel in some magical way that they are. That is one of the greatest problems that confronts a therapist in dealing with these situations. If they are not handled appropriately, the child's sense of guilt may manifest itself in one of two ways. She may begin to act out in a negative way, that is, not be able to enjoy sex as an adult. Or, even more commonly, she may act out as if this is the way she has always been and she might as well make the most of it. These girls frequently wind up as prostitutes or, at the very least, extremely promiscuous. Wendy was clearly heading in that direction, as the court had already indicated. At seventeen, she had begun to charge for her sexual favors; feeling that she had deserved it, she said, "I might as well play the game, I've got the name anyway."

Even in cases where the young woman who has been molested as a child doesn't become a prostitute, she may have distorted views about sex and children. In her own marriage, her children may themselves be exploited by a parent. As noted before, this is often the result of physical abuse and of sexual abuse as well. Almost every case of sexual abuse has its antecedents in the parents having had the same kind of experiences.

Psychiatry is learning more and more about this kind of behavior as the problems come out into the open. More and more clinics and centers are being established where people can deal with these problems in an open and unashamed manner. A recent example of such facilities is the Barbara Sinatra Center for Children in Rancho Mirage, California. Part of the Eisenhower Medical Center, it is dedicated to the evaluation and treatment of young people and children who have been sexually abused or molested. The goal is to enable them to understand and deal with their problems openly and to help them to work out guidelines and solutions to resolve the situation.

Often, outside help is essential to resolve these problems. If the family is left to its own devices, the situation only gets worse. The outside help may be in the form of a formal clinic or informal relationships in the community with teachers, guidance counselors, mental health professionals, or other family members.

These are extremely difficult cases, and unless they are handled properly the results can be disastrous. The experience at the Barbara Sinatra Center is that in many cases a reunion of the family can be achieved. The children are frequently placed in a foster home while the parents try to work out their problems with each other. The children receive group or individual therapy to help them understand that the problems are not of their making. The parents also take part in individual or group therapy situations where they can understand that they themselves were probably either molested or involved in violent situations in childhood and can come to recognize their own culpability, guilt, and responsibility in these situations. As a result of the counseling process, in many cases the family can be reunited.

In addition to methods of treating people who have been victims of this most violent kind of assault, that is, sexual attack, there are other ways to deal with the overall problem. The best, clearly, is to avoid it in the first place. There are guidelines to prevent the problem, some of the most appropriate of which relate primarily to awareness. The possibility of this kind of behavior occurring should be considered from the outset. A mother should be aware that her husband may not always be a model of virtue and high thinking. She must be especially concerned if he drinks too much or uses drugs, both of which tend to dissolve moral inhibitions and cause the acting out of unconscious sexual wishes. This is especially so in marriages in which the husband is not the natural father of the children and may therefore have less inhibition in the first place. In either case, however, the use of drugs and alcohol can give the person an excuse to stop controlling his fantasies and to act them out in a destructive way.

Another extremely important way to avoid the problem is to have a positive relationship between parents and children. If parents and children can communicate freely and openly, not only can sexual problems be handled more satisfactorily, but all of the other things that come up and cause difficulty can be laid on the table. This is clearly the case in sexual matters, however, because when children feel that they can communicate freely and openly, they are able to talk about small things before they become major issues. Many of the problems that arise can be nipped in the bud. If the father or stepfather or other adult starts to be interested in a child sexually, it can be discussed. The opening overtures can be brought up by the young child. He or she can mention it to the other parent and discuss it freely with siblings. Often the father or stepfather makes overtures to a child before he risks an overt move. If the child is able to report this to the mother and she has faith enough in the child to listen, the mother can inform her husband that she is aware of what is going on and let him know that it is totally unacceptable. That can frequently be enough to stop his explorations. It might even be enough, if it happens more than once, to force him to look further into himself and get the kind of help he needs.

If a sexual abuse situation arises for an adolescent, the same kind of guidelines can be applied. The young person should be able to talk to the mother or father about the advances of the opposite parent at the very beginning of the behavior. If a parent is drinking or using drugs, someone else should be informed. If both parents are doing so and, therefore, give license to each other to act inappropriately sexually, a third party should be consulted: a grandparent, an aunt, an uncle, or one of the other resources mentioned earlier. Adolescents and young people must know that the resources are available and that they will be listened to. Once that happens, the problem can be addressed and, more often than not, successfully handled.

Sexual abuse is a major health problem that is only now becoming the subject of our awareness. The opening of the Barbara Sinatra Center is just one of the many moves that our communities are taking to cope with it. Because of the greater degree of openness in dealing with sexual matters, child abuse, and family problems in general, they can now come to the surface and be handled in the proper manner. In the long run, this kind of frankness can lead to a more positive growth for children and young adults. It can help to avoid many of the frightening, overwhelming, and depressing situations that otherwise persist into adult life for victims who remain unnoticed and untreated.

As in any other significant health problem, early consultation with an expert in the field is essential. But even before that, awareness on the part of the individual and the family is the primary step. You can't deal with a problem that you don't recognize. If you have questions, talk to someone. Sometimes even talking to a friend can clarify the situation. If you don't have someone that you think is knowledgeable, seek someone out. Professional people are able to keep secrets. If they feel that there is nothing there to worry about, they will tell you so. If they think there are other moves that you need to make, they will tell you that too. The main thing is to ask the question and then consider the impact of the answer.

CHAPTER X

"I'm Not a Bad Guy"

"All I ever tried to do was be friendly. I'm not a bad guy, I just like little boys. I'm really a nice guy."

This "nice guy" was arrested for lewd and lascivious behavior with a ten-year-old boy, who was his girlfriend's child. He was facing felony charges in Superior Court. His attorney had referred him to a psychiatrist for evaluation and treatment. The intent was to find some psychological reason for his behavior to offer the court, in the hope of avoiding the heavy penalties, including a prison sentence, that might result from conviction of the charges.

Unfortunately, this was not an unusual case. The courts frequently see adult men who have been arrested for molesting young boys and performing sexual acts with them. Usually the act is oral copulation: the young boy being asked to copulate with the adult male or vice versa.

Most of the time these men are not seen by psychiatrists, as they cannot afford either a private attorney or psychiatric evaluation and treatment. Unless the offender is grossly disturbed and therefore unable to assist in his own defense or understand the charges, the Public Defender's office has neither the time nor the funding to enter into studies of pedophiles. Nevertheless, they are definitely sick men. An understanding of these situations is important to prevent them from happening and even more so, to help the victim to deal with his feelings. If we can understand an illness, we are in a far better position to prevent it than if we only find it and try to clear up the mess afterwards. But cleaning up the mess *is* essential and must be considered.

Men who seek sexual activity with young boys tend to be interested primarily in boys before they reach puberty and start to show secondary sex characteristics. They are not much interested in boys who start to have deeper voices, develop pubic hair, and otherwise appear to be more adult than child. This gives us a clue to the thinking and the mental distortions of the pedophile. He is fearful of contact with both adult women and adult men. He prefers prepubescent boys who offer no threat to him physically, sexually, or emotionally.

How he finds these boys and how he gets them to cooperate is part of society's problem. Unfortunately, there are too many young boys who can be seduced. We probably all remember the warnings our parents gave us when we were little: "Don't take candy from strangers." "Don't take presents from strangers." "Don't talk to people you don't know." When I was a young boy I assumed that my parents were trying to protect me from kidnapping, although why anybody would want to kidnap a boy from a working-class family was not clear to me. In retrospect, I realize that adults can want to have something to do with little children besides hold them for ransom.

By the very nature of their age, young children are extremely naive. They don't know much about the world or what is going on around them. They tend to think that all people who are nice to them are doing so for altruistic reasons. When a man comes along and offers to buy them a candy bar or a comic book or take them for a ride, they tend to take him at face value. If their parents aren't around, they might very well go along.

Even then, the pedophile is very careful. He doesn't want to get involved with a boy who will "tell on him." He feels out the situation and tries to see if the boy is interested in being friendly, perhaps in going to an amusement park, to the beach, or to the movies. The pedophile acts in a way that will allay the suspicions of the child so that even if the parents talk to the child, he appears to be open, aboveboard, and simply a "nice man."

Sometimes parents are just as gullible as their children. A busy mother with more than one child might welcome the interest and attention of a well-dressed, educated, and apparently well-meaning man who wants to befriend her son. Maybe she is divorced or separated and doesn't have a man around to help with the children. Maybe she is low on funds and just managing to scrape by when some nice gentleman offers to take her child to Disneyland, a picture show, or even to McDonald's for a "Big Mac."

In the most extreme cases, it appears that the parent or parents are not actually naive, but in some way are accomplices of the pedophile. That is, they almost unconsciously go along with the design of the child molester to achieve some short-term gain. They want to have the child taken off their hands, or amused, or to have the molester buy the child clothing or other things they can't afford. It is almost as if they are selling the child to him for a rather small price.

In most cases, the child is very naive. He only knows what he has learned of the world from his parents and from other adults. If he is seven, eight, or nine years old, he hasn't had a chance to become "street wise." If the adult male wants to hug and kiss him, he sees it as a sign of affection not unlike that of his father, uncle, or grandparent. Sometimes the man *is* a stepfather, an adoptive parent, or an uncle. When the man wants to touch the boy's genitals, it usually feels good and probably seems just another expression of affection.

Eventually, when the pedophile wants to look at his genitals or share looking at each other's genitals, the child thinks that this is the way things are done when you become "good friends" with someone else. If the man has been kind and generous to the child and tells him that he would rather "keep this a secret between us," the child almost always goes along. It is only later that he begins to develop a sense of guilt or a feeling that something is not right. If may be only when the child becomes pubescent and starts talking to other kids that he discovers what really has been going on. By then, it is too late. Guilt, shame, and a feeling of being bad can overwhelm him. Many young boys who are led into pedophilic activities by unscrupulous adults find the guilt and the negative feelings so overwhelming that they themselves are pushed into similar activities or even become young male prostitutes.

Obviously, the stigma and the blame have to be laid at the feet of the adult who sets these children up. There is also some responsibility on the part of the parent who has looked the other way or been unconcerned or even unconsciously assisted in the activity. Efforts to educate parents are very important. But even more, we need to pay early attention to the victim of these acts. We must work with him to relieve his guilt before these activities become part of his life.

Perhaps specific instances will shed some light upon the activities of the pedophile and how to understand him and possibly deal with this perversion.

Arthur A. was a successful businessman who consulted a doctor at the request of his attorney because of an arrest for child molestation. He had been arrested on the complaint of his girlfriend, the mother of a ten-year-old boy, who had finally realized that her son's trips with Arthur to Disneyland and Knott's Berry Farm and the movies and restaurants were not all on the up and up. She began to question her son more closely about what they did on these trips and eventually discovered that Arthur's interest in her son was more than being "a big brother." His interest, in point of fact, was explicitly sexual and took the form of frequent oral copulation. When she had established this clearly, despite her closeness to Arthur, she filed a complaint with the local police. They investigated the situation, someone from the Child Protective Service interviewed the boy, and eventually the District Attorney charged Arthur on multiple counts of child molestation.

Arthur retained a criminal lawyer and pleaded not guilty. Nevertheless, it became quite clear that boys were Arthur's sexual preference and interest. A prominent thirty-five-year-old business executive, he had never been married, and he dated only for show. He had a steady girlfriend to keep up appearances in the community.

As a child, Arthur had grown up in a family in which his father had had polio and was unable to walk without crutches and braces. His mother was the breadwinner and a powerful and overwhelming figure. Arthur had fantasies as a child that his mother had actually caused his father's disability. He believed that he had to be very careful so that the mother wouldn't visit the same kind of punishment upon him. He wasn't sure what it was that he shouldn't do, but it was probably safer to stay away from his mother and people like her if he could. At the same time, he was shown a lot of affection and attention by one of his mother's brothers who lived with the family. When the uncle drank a great deal he became extremely demonstrative with Arthur. Since Arthur's dad was uninterested in anything because of his self-pity and feelings of inadequacy, Arthur welcomed the contact with Uncle Fred. Uncle Fred when drinking became increasingly affectionate, began fondling Arthur's genitals, and established sexual contact with him. Eventually, Arthur's dad discovered what was going on, and Uncle Fred had to leave the household.

As Arthur later recalled, however, "Uncle Fred was probably the closest person to me in my life, and I really was sorry when he left." He had a warm and personal relationship with Fred that was never to be duplicated, even though he tried in high school and college to date and to get close to women. "There was always something that held me back." He never really felt close to women and was always afraid of being rejected and hurt. He made a try at getting engaged on one occasion, but he was really panicky, and eventually both he and the girl agreed that it would never work out. Arthur was bright and had established his own business and made himself a success far greater than his father or mother had dreamed he could do. With success came money, a nice house, and a car, but no one to share them with.

Arthur never forgot Uncle Fred and how close he had felt to him. Finally, he began making little overtures to the young son of a gardener who came in several times a week to take care of his property. The boy was about the age Arthur had been when Uncle Fred had played with him. Arthur used to bring the boy candy bars and once in a while gave him an ice cream bar from the freezer. The gardener thought this was fine. Later, when Arthur offered to take the boy for a ride downtown, the gardener still thought it was fine. The relationship continued, and eventually Arthur again experienced the warm feelings that he had known with Uncle Fred, but this time he was "Uncle Fred" and the young child was he.

It seemed to Arthur that it worked the same in both directions. It was "the closest thing I had ever felt." Arthur insisted that it wasn't simply sexual release that he sought, but an emotional experience that he had never been able to have with a woman.

Eventually, as usually happens in these situations, the gardener found out when his son made a slip in discussing some of their activities. The father pressed the matter further and went to Arthur's house one day for a confrontation. Arthur tried to deny what had happened, but the gardener was not satisfied, and a loud argument ensued. Fortunately for Arthur, there were other people in the neighborhood, and the gardener left in a rage, threatening that he would "one day get you." That was the end of that relationship. Later, Arthur made other contacts and on several occasions was able to get out of trouble by buying off the parents with gifts: a car one time and several thousand dollars another. Finally, he ran into a mother who wasn't interested in that kind of exchange.

After extensive psychiatric evaluation and testing, it became clear that Arthur in reality was still a prepubescent boy. He had never matured emotionally. He was still afraid of his mother and, by extension, of all women. He had what Freud described as "castration anxiety." By that Freud meant the fear of many young children that they will be castrated if they try to have sexual relations with their mother. Usually this fear is related to the father's jealousy. Arthur had felt that his mother had physically crippled his father for getting close to her, and he was afraid of trying it himself. By extension, therefore, he could not get close to any woman. The next best solution was the same kind of relationship that he and Uncle Fred had experienced.

Since it was Arthur's first arrest, the court was lenient. He was placed on probation and ordered to undergo extensive and intensive psychiatric treatment, including aversion therapy.

Aversion therapy involved the use of movies and slides of attractive young boys chosen by Arthur himself. Upon viewing a slide, Arthur would be given a small electric shock, which continued as long as he kept looking at the picture on the projector. Eventually, to stop the discomfort of the electric shock, he would switch to another picture. That picture would be a neutral scene, or perhaps a heterosexual scene, and there would be no shock attached. He could look at the picture for a while and then click to the next. Each time he came to a picture of a sexual nature involving a young child, the electric shock would begin after one second and would stop only when he changed the picture. Aversion therapy has proved successful in several areas, such as sexual perversions and alcoholism.

Arthur remained on probation and under treatment for two years. At that time the psychiatrist told the court that he believed that Arthur was free of his sexual interests. Whether this was actually the case several years later is not certain. Arthur has not returned for treatment and has not appeared in court for the same offense.

As has been said, the problem of dealing with the victim of the pedophile is important and crucial. A ten-year-old boy can be mentally scarred for the rest of his life if something is not done to help him deal with the feelings created by the sexual experiences he has had.

In this particular case, Charles, the victim of Arthur's attention, needed a lot of assistance. Charles had at first seen Arthur as a trusted and valuable friend. After all, he was his mother's good friend and had been with her for a long time; he seemed almost like a substitute father. When Arthur began his advances, Charles had believed that this was the way things were supposed to be between a boy and his substitute father. When Arthur showed Charles that it was pleasurable to have sexual feelings from touching genitals, Charles thought that was O.K. It was only later, as their relations became more intimate, that he began to have vague suspicions. He never heard his friends at school talk about their dads doing the things that Arthur did with him. It was true that their dads sometimes took them to Disneyland or on picnics or to the beach, but Charles never heard them talk about the other things.

Charles never heard the other boys say that their dads liked to take showers with them. He never heard them talk about experiences with their dads when they would play with each other's genitals. They really didn't know anything about how a man's penis gets hard and ejaculation occurs when you play with it. They had some vague ideas about this and masturbation that they talked about, but never with their dads.

Charles thought there was something the matter, but he was afraid to say anything. He valued his relationship with Arthur; Arthur was so good to him and kept telling him that he loved him. Arthur was good. He bought him presents and clothes and took him to all kinds of nice places. His mom went out with Arthur too. Maybe Arthur did things with her that they weren't supposed to talk about. He wasn't sure.

"I was scared to tell my mom about what Arthur and I did. She never told me anything that she did with Arthur when they were alone, so I figured that was the kind of thing you weren't supposed to talk about. When I asked Arthur about it, he told me that I was right. He said I should never tell my mom about it, that this was just something between us. It was our secret and something that I didn't have to tell anybody. He even told me I shouldn't tell my friends, because they wouldn't understand. They weren't as close to their dads as I was to Arthur. I thought that was kind of strange, but Arthur said so and I figured it was O.K.''

Charles was finally able to confide some of his doubts and fears to the therapist whom he met at the Child Guidance Center. It was important for him to have someone to talk to outside of the family to unload these feelings. He needed a nonjudgmental adult to listen to him and to tell him that he was all right. It was important that someone reassure him that he didn't do anything wrong. Arthur had been arrested, and Charles had had to go and talk to the judge. They even had Charles make some video tapes about what had gone on. They were all very nice to him, but he knew there was something ''really wrong'' in what had been going on. He was filled with ideas that he was bad and had done something terrible. He was just learning about ''queers.'' The kids in school talked about them and ''fags'' a lot. Charles was beginning to think that maybe that's what Arthur was and he too. It required a great deal of reassurance by the therapist to help him deal with these feelings.

Charles was being treated by a male therapist. This was so that he would understand that boys could have close and friendly relationships with men that didn't involve physical contact.

Charles and his therapist sometimes went across the

street from the clinic to the supermarket to buy an ice cream bar. Occasionally, they took walks in the nearby park, but there wasn't any of the touching and affection that he had experienced with Arthur. He admitted that he missed that a lot, but he came to learn that it was best for him to find the affection he needed in a verbal way and that physical contact between men should be limited to hugging or shaking hands or reassuring each other, without sexual or genital contact.

The main goal of the therapy was to relieve Charles of his guilt. It was terribly important for him to feel that he was a normal kid and would be able to grow up like all of his friends. The episode with Arthur was going to be something in the past. It would eventually have to be seen as someone else's mistake that caused Charles some difficulty. It would have to be viewed as if it were an auto accident or some other event that Charles didn't control but that he had to deal with.

"After all, if I were in a car and it crashed and I got hurt, it wouldn't be my fault, would it?" queried Charles. When his therapist agreed and told him that he was in essence the victim of someone else's problem, he began to accept it. It took many months and even now Charles keeps in touch with a therapist. He is also part of a group of kids who have had similar experiences, who get together and talk. This is a form of group therapy in which victims are able to talk about their feelings and drain them off.

The number of people who are victims of this kind of sexual abuse is surprising. Many people go through childhood and adolescence and early adult life without ever telling anybody about such experiences. The real danger is that they will begin to think there is something wrong with them. They will start to act ''queer'' or have some other aberration that they can't control and that overwhelms them. The earlier one can deal with this, the more effective treatment can be.

Nevertheless, if you have had an experience like this, or if you know someone who has, it is *never* too late to do something about it. Even when you are fifteen or eighteen or twenty-five, you can get help. There is someone who will understand and be able to talk to you and help you to realize that you are not always the center of the universe. Everything that you do and that is done to you is not always your fault. Sometimes things happen to us that are beyond our control. In cases like that, it's very important to have a friend who can help you, but professional help is essential.

It is always good to have buddies and friends that you can talk to, but in a situation of this nature, a professional person is needed. If you know of someone with such a problem, you should certainly advise him of this and tell him where he can find help. If you don't know a particular place, you can direct him to his family doctor or the school counselor or one of the teachers who might be of help. Sometimes the boy's parents can help if they are able to deal with the situation calmly. Many times when parents discover that their child has been sexually abused they become enraged and try to take the law into their own hands. That, of course, is illegal even with the best of motivations. We cannot take vigilante action. Even in these terrible situations, the law is the course of action that is essential.

Violence takes many forms. In this book we have discussed physical violence and mental violence and, in this chapter and the previous one, sexual violence. Any kind of violence must be avoided.

Until a very short time ago in the span of human existence on this planet, people lived under primitive and difficult conditions. Violence is a part of the human experience. It is a part that we have to learn to control. It is no longer necessary to be violent to survive. We don't live in jungles anymore. We don't have to fight wild animals or struggle with each other for food. We don't need to capture a mate from a rival by violent means. We have to learn to deal with violence wherever it appears by using reason rather than emotion. The human brain is the one thing that distinguishes us from the other animals on our planet. We have to learn to use it more effectively, or we will be destroyed by our violent instincts. Violence in the family is probably the closest to home, the most destructive, and the thing that we have to cope with most intensively.

CHAPTER XI

Putting It Together

As we have indicated elsewhere in this book, no form of violence is any longer acceptable in human behavior. We have established a United Nations to avoid violence among countries. In our own country the FBI and other groups try to prevent crime on a national scale. Within our states, state and local police and other groups work to prevent and control violent behavior among people. The essence of a civilized society is to avoid solving problems through physical actions such as rage and assault. Sometimes the violence that occurs within a family escapes the notice of the rest of the *Conclusion* world because it is contained and can be covered up or hidden from the authorities. That doesn't make it any more acceptable or any less dangerous. In many ways, it makes it worse. It is our job to try to deal with it as effectively as we can.

The very fact that you have taken up this book and read it indicates that you are concerned with and interested in this problem. You may have a friend, a relative, or someone close to you who is involved in a problem of this nature, or it may affect you yourself. Whatever the circumstance, it is important that you are concerned and that you do something about it.

We have seen that violence within families takes many

forms. A teenage mother can be pushed by the stress and pressures of her life into violence and behavior she cannot control. She may be pressed into actually striking and injuring her own child. Such behavior can actually result in the death of an infant. A baby is very fragile and could easily be injured by a mother out of control or filled with rage and despair. And, of course, the mother's life would be scarred forever.

We have also described cases of young people who were attacked and injured by those who are supposed to love them. Parents sometimes maim and victimize their own children. This sometimes results in the children's being sent to foster homes or to live with relatives in other towns. Often alcohol or other drugs are involved. Such behavior can be the result of the parents' own internal problems and can even be traced back in time to the fact that they themselves were abused physically and exposed to violence when they were children. Whatever the reason, the children are indeed victimized and can suffer as a result for the rest of their lives.

We have talked about how divorce and marital separation can lead to fighting and how the entire family can be sucked into the most violent confrontations as a result. Sometimes the young people believe that they are responsible for the actions of their entire family, and they begin to feel guilty about the behavior of others. The divorce or separation sometimes results in actual fighting between mother and father and can wind up in bitter and lifelong feuds within the family.

As you will recall, there is something common to all of these happenings and experiences. Not only these, but the rivalry between siblings, the jealousy of children for parental affection, and the fights between brother and brother, sister and sister, and close relatives have a common thread. That thread is the reversion to primitive reactions, rather than reliance upon reason. As we have seen, the primitive mind relies upon violence to solve problems; the civilized mind relies upon thinking, reason, and intelligence.

Sometimes the problems are technical or medical ones, like the attention deficit disorder described earlier. These medical problems, like juvenile diabetes, cerebral palsy, and even schizophrenia, cause behavioral changes that are beyond the individual's control and can only be understood and handled by a physician. Nevertheless, what appears on the surface is bizarre activity or possibly violence on the part of the young person and sometimes violent reaction to the child because of the family's misunderstanding, anger, or impatience.

Obviously, help must be sought out in these situations and competent professionals consulted.

Sometimes problems are brought about by severe illness or other distortions in the personality of family members. Occasionally, they may try to use alcohol as their excuse. Usually, however, even when sober they fantasize or imagine violent activity, assault against friends, relatives, wives, husbands, and their own children. The alcohol then is just an excuse, the solvent that dissolves their inhibitions, their conscience, and their judgment. Alcohol is never an excuse; it is only an ingredient that makes things worse.

Many sexual violations that occur can be just as damaging and violent in their effect upon the victim as the physical beatings and batterings that people can inflict upon each other. Not only are these sexual assaults dangerous to the child in his long-term growth and development, but they are also destructive to the uninvolved parent and to the perpetrator of the acts. Guilt, shame, feelings of inadequacy and incompetence are all part of the price that people pay for sexual violence, incest, pedophilia, and sexual molestation.

Each chapter has set forth ways in which a person might handle such problems should they come up in his or her own life or in the life of someone he knows. Some general guidelines exist that can be followed in attempting to understand all of these problems, and some general approaches that are important to understand and review. Some situations are not as clear-cut or as obvious as those we have described. Something may be a little different from what we have discussed, and it is important to know how to proceed in that situation as well.

I. The first thing to do is *RECOGNIZE THE BEHAVIOR*.

It is important not to mistake other kinds of behavior for violence. Sometimes petty incidents can be blown up out of proportion. Verbal fights and disagreements between brother and sister do not always mean a violent confrontation. Reprimands don't always mean that a parent is about to assault a child; even physical spanking of small children does not necessarily constitute physical violence.

Affection between mother and child or father and child is important and even essential to growth. Therefore, if a father embraces his daughter it doesn't mean that he is molesting her sexually. We have to accept that there are reasonable limits for all behavior, and only when a person steps beyond those limits do we need to become concerned.

Thus it is important to recognize when behavior is beyond the pale or so obviously abnormal that something must be done.

II. If you believe that you see or have become part of the real thing, it becomes important to *VALIDATE THE BEHAVIOR*. be sure it is violent

By that we mean to make sure that the behavior is, in fact, excessive and violent to the extent that it can be dangerous to the victim as well as to the perpetrator. When behavior reaches such proportions, it becomes important to consult books such as this one and other resource materials. It is usually worthwhile to talk to a trusted friend or someone who has experience in these areas. You don't have to be specific about who or what is involved. If you just discuss the topic in general, you can get some feeling as to the opinion of others as to the degree to which the behavior may be away from the normal.

III. Once you are certain, or at least reasonably certain, that the behavior is abnormal and excessively violent, you need to *CONFRONT THOSE INVOLVED*.

That means it is necessary to discuss—either with the victim if you are a relative or a friend, or with the others involved if you are a principal in the problem—

why you feel that the behavior is abnormal and what you think should be done about it.

These three steps are essential to deal with the problem, and only after you carry them out should you proceed to the next level of activity.

1. *TALKING.* Sometimes (and this is the rarest of solutions) people are able to alter their behavior when someone simply points it out to them. They may be able to understand that it is inappropriate and destructive when you let them know that others are aware that they are doing it. This certainly should be the first step to take. If you can talk to the person involved, point out the error of his or her ways, and ask if he will consider change, you might be able to save a lot of pain and heartache and destruction. If you have a friend who is so involved, you can suggest to him or her that you would be willing to listen. Even though you're not an expert you might have some helpful thoughts and ideas about it. This is a valuable first step. It may be the crucial step in solving the problem.

talk about problem

2. *EXPERIENCED OTHERS.* Many people who are not experts in mental health, social relationships, medical diseases, sexual activity, or child-parent relations have lived in the world for years and are able to use their experience constructively. These people may be uninvolved relatives such as grandparents, uncles, aunts, or cousins. Most of us have relatives, either in our own town or nearby, whom we can call upon from time to time if for no other help than verbal assistance. If there is no such person, or if such a person is not understanding or wants to deny the problem, other

call the experts

trusted adult members of the community can be consulted. Sometimes a neighbor or a family friend is willing to talk and think about and deal with problems among friends.   *Seek advice from teachers*

3. *EDUCATORS.* Teachers frequently encounter problems among families and are consulted by young men and women in their classes. If there is a teacher whom you trust or who you think is knowledgeable, understanding, and willing to listen, he or she can be an invaluable resource. Many teachers are thoughtful, understanding, and discreet. They will listen to your story and tell you whether or not they think it deserves further investigation.

A recent survey indicated that athletic coaches are the people that students consult the most often on personal problems. This is not hard to understand, since coaches are usually the closest to teenagers, especially in situations in which there is family discord. You can talk to the coach whether you are a boy or a girl and get the benefit of his or her experience in life. Coaches are teachers besides being athletic experts, and they have a lot of experience in the world and in dealing with young people. The same is true, of course, of school counselors. These people in many states are trained in the areas of psychology, human interrelationships, and emotional problems. They can be called upon for more than simply discussing what courses to take, what career to pursue, or what college to attend.

4. *SPIRITUAL EXPERTS.* Religious counseling has been the resort of troubled people for thousands of years. People have always turned to ministers, priests, and rabbis for guidance. These professionals are used to

hearing about problems. They have dedicated their lives to helping other people and dealing with their problems. Most of the time, they try to be nonjudgmental in their attitude. Occasionally that may not be the case, and other resources have to sought. Nevertheless, if you have a religious background or know someone whom you feel you can trust and who is kind and wise, religious counseling is a valuable resource.

5. *MEDICAL PROFESSIONALS*. Every town and city across the country has family doctors, general practitioners, nurses, internists, and other doctors who have spent their lives dealing with people. They are used to dealing with families and family problems and have no moral scruples about talking about such issues in privacy and with discretion. They are professionals yet, at the same time, understand people's need for privacy. They are aware of the resources available in the community but often are able within their own resources to give guidance and assistance. Sometimes they have enough authority and stature to get someone to change his or her behavior because they say so. Other times, they engage in counseling themselves. Most family doctors and general practitioners are adept at this kind of counseling, and many of them have nurse practitioners and other staff members who can be of help. This is a valuable resource and available in almost every community. It should be considered when you are looking for help.

6. *MENTAL HEALTH PROFESSIONALS*. There is a growing availability of experts in the field of family violence and sexual abuse. Many larger communities

and counties have Child Guidance Centers and Family Counseling Centers that are becoming more and more experienced in the areas of family violence, marital discord, sexual abuse, and child abuse. They have mental health counselors, psychologists, nurses, social workers, and psychiatrists. Many centers are funded by counties and states and therefore need not charge large fees. There are, of course, private practitioners who do charge fees and are available for the same purposes.

All of these people have dedicated their lives to understanding human behavior, to dealing with human frailties, and to guiding others toward building their lives in positive directions rather than negative ones.

7. *GOVERNMENTAL AGENCIES.* If all else fails, governmental resources can be used. Every community has an Office of the District Attorney or a Prosecutor's Office to deal with people who have committed violent crimes. Most families are reluctant to call on these people, but they do exist and can be summoned for help. The Office of the Prosecutor or District Attorney knows whom to call in other government agencies and can invoke the services of the county Child Protective Services. A community welfare agency or other group may be able to help families in distress.

Often, the other people whom we have described above have to call in the county authorities, the police, the district attorney, or others if their efforts are of no avail. They must call in the authorities when they perceive violence to a minor child, since that is the law in most states. That doesn't mean that they can't continue their guidance and counseling, but the law does require this kind of intervention to protect those who may not be able to protect themselves.

It is essential to understand that problems of family violence are potentially the most destructive in our society. They create long-term damage that sometimes goes from one generation to the next. But most important, they can be avoided.

If you are aware of such a problem in your own family or involving a friend or relative, it is important for you to deal with it. You are not being a squealer or a stool pigeon when you do so. You are serving the family, the friends, the people you love the most when you try to help them. It is much the same as if you were the first to see a fire in a theater. To do nothing would be a crime. To start to deal with the fire before it spreads is the obvious course of action. That is the same kind of action that must be taken in family violence. Doing the right thing may seem hard sometimes, but in the long run it is easier than doing nothing. It is easier than living with a guilty conscience. It is easier than observing the tragic results of inactivity in later years.

It has been said that evil flourishes when good men sit idly by. Violence is evil, and it will flourish if the good people among us don't do anything to counteract it. The reader of this book obviously wants to do good, or he wouldn't have picked up the book in the first place. If you can act upon these principles, you will ensure for yourself a sense of well-being and tranquility. You may also help others now and for generations in the future.

Index

T